# FROM MIME TO SIGN

by

**GILBERT C. EASTMAN**

with

Martin Noretsky
Sharon Censoplano

T·J·PUBLISHERS

T.J. Publishers, Inc.
817 Silver Spring Ave., 206
Silver Spring, MD 20910

ISBN #0-932666-34-5 paper
ISBN #0-932666-38-8 hard cover

# Acknowledgement

**From Mime to Sign** is based on the ideas that have been evolving for more than twenty years. In 1987, Ramon Rodriguez and Terrence J. O'Rourke of T.J. Publishers assembled a team that analyzed these ideas, restructured them, and translated them into the book you have in your hands.

The publisher and authors wish to thank the following people who contributed to this team effort:

Frieda Henry and Spence Carter, photographers, for their skill in capturing motion in a still medium;

Nina Kuch, visual editor, for drawing on her knowledge of visual perception and learning to create a balance between text and visuals that are readable, clear, and concise;

Carolyn Robel, graphic designer, for creating a consistent and pleasing layout;

Pat McNees for her careful editing of the manuscript and her valuable comments about its content;

and the many students who have enrolled in Visual-Gestural Communication at Gallaudet University—and in workshops throughout the country—whose enthusiasm and feedback over the years have contributed enormously to **From Mime to Sign.**

# Table of Contents

# Foreword

Nothing like this book has ever been seen before. Books about sign language and how-to-do-it books have been around for a long time, but Gil Eastman starts where the action is, representing things and feelings so that someone else can see them. Your ordinary sign language book starts with words and tries to tell you how to shape your hands and move them to make a sign that will stand for each word. Gil shows you how to make your thoughts and emotions visible with your body, hands, and face.

Scholarly sign language text books set out to prove that American Sign Language really is a language. Gil already knows it is, and before you realize what is happening he has you using your face and hands the way good signers do without talking about grammar or structure. His photographs and exercises reveal a very special art, the art of mime, the performer who can move you by telling stories without using any words.

That is how sign language begins. It is not just another language with rules and vocabulary to memorize. Sign language is a way of expressing with your body, instead of your voice, what you have to say along with the appropriate feelings. Before you get to signs as language, as you work through Gil's chapters, you will become more and more adept in expressing your thoughts and feelings without using your voice. At first you will work with representing things in two dimensions, circles and squares and zig-zag lines. This is already something new: spoken languages work with only one dimension; their sounds occur one after the other on a line through time. However, two-dimensional pictures are only the start.

Soon Gil will have you using three dimensions, making circles into balls and balloons and squares into boxes. Stick with him and you will learn how to use all four dimensions, the three dimensions of space and the time dimension as well—one sign with another. And that too is how a sign language works, because it is the way the master sense of human vision works.

Ideas and books as original as this one don't just happen. Besides teaching mime and sign, Gil creates, produces, directs, and acts in plays and teaches others the arts of the theater. The pictures in this book explain his success: he teaches what no one else knows quite so well how to do. But don't get the idea that this is just a book about technique. These days how to package messages gets a lot of attention, but this book starts with the message's sender, a human being in full view. Like a mime, a signer has only the human body to work with, but he also has the potential of the human mind. The greatness of mimes like Charlie Chaplin and Marcel Marceau is as much in what they are expressing as in their skill at expressing it.

Gil's knowledge of the world's great dramatic literature is behind his carefully developed gift of making the classics seem brand new when expressed on stage without spoken words. Actors in the original National Theater of the Deaf learned from Gil. Sign language poets have profited from his course in "Mime to Sign." I do not know how many of the brilliant student leaders of the "Deaf President Now" movement in March of 1988 have studied with Gil, but he has been at Gallaudet University for a generation, and the spirit of this book, how to put the exact idea and the appropriate reaction into full view, is something in the air of the place now.

Of course this book will not make a reader who studies it and practices all its exercises into a Sophocles or a Shakespeare, or a Chaplin or a Marceau, or a Hlibok or a Rarus—unless that reader has greatness in him or her. It can do what learning another language sometimes does, enlarge and enrich experience; but it will do more. Learning a new language in the silent dimensions that mimes and deaf signers use will open a new dimension of life. Study with Gil and you will see better. You and your ideas will look better too.

**William C. Stokoe**
Washington, D.C.

**Welcome**

esture, mime and facial expression are the fundamentals of American Sign Language. You are familiar with many of these aspects of visual communication and, in fact, are already using them. Did anyone ever walk up to you for example, and ask you why you're so happy or what's wrong? You never said a word, but your facial expression said it for you.

You probably already use some gestures and mime effectively, too. Have you ever been at a party and gestured to someone across the room to see if they wanted something to drink, or eat, or to ask them to come over to where you were? We propose to develop what you already do naturally into the basic skills needed for American Sign Language.

**From Mime to Sign** guides you along a natural path of instruction toward effective sign language skills. Drawing on familiar gestures and facial expressions, beginning immediately in Chapter One, we ask you to think more visually, in pictures instead of words. Chapters Two through Five teach you the skills you need to create and place objects within a scene.

We will ask you to begin by creating simple two-dimensional designs—using your fingers, hands and body and the space around you as a painter uses paint, brushes and canvas. Then you will add depth to your gestures, the depth that turns a circle into a ball, or a balloon.

You will learn that in gesturing a scene, each piece of the picture must be put in its proper place. You will also learn more than fifty facial expressions that add different shades of meaning to your gestures.

Once you are able to create objects, you will learn to use them while doing an activity. In Chapter Six you will show people and objects in action through mime and begin to integrate your skills in gesture, mime and facial expression. Chapter Seven will provide you with techniques for simplifying action sequences by using your hands and fingers—instead of your whole body—to communicate people in action.

Not all scenes are limited to one person or one item, so you will learn how to create multiples of both people and objects in Chapter Eight. Chapter Nine expands your horizons into the great outdoors. Here you will create an outdoor environment that includes animals and birds.

In Chapter Ten you apply everything you have learned by telling both short and long stories. By the time you reach the Epilogue: The Design of a Sign, you will be amazed at the amount of sign language you have acquired simply by practicing natural gestures, mime and facial expressions.

So, if you've always wanted to know sign language, but thought it would be too hard to learn—relax—and let FROM MIME TO SIGN guide you in a manner that takes advantage of what you already know and encourages you to continue—naturally.

# Chapter 1
# Deja Vu
## Applying What You Already Know

tart with what you know. The content of **From Mime to Sign** is firmly based on theory and years of experience and observation, but it emphasizes ''doing.'' In Chapter One you will start communicating with gestures, mime and facial expressions that seem easy and familiar.

The illustrations in this book have been carefully selected to show you step by step what to do to become skilled in thinking in pictures. The illustrations themselves are examples of how pictures express meaning. You will frequently see paired photographs that are meant to be read as the first and last positions of a movement. The first pair of photographs below show a door. The sequence starts with the door closed and ends with the door in the open position.

Sometimes clarity requires a middle position. You may see a photographic sequence of three or more photographs. The following series shows the gestures for a table. In this situation, read the photographs sequentially from the first through the last.

In longer sequences the context will tell you whether the pictures are to be read as solo shots or as a pair or series.

Try reading the following example of "driving" a car. Can you identify the two photograph sequence of fastening the seatbelt? Do you see the photograph that expresses adjusting the rear view mirror? Can you find the one for turning the ignition key? To express the idea of "drive" you may add gestures showing the hood, roof, trunk and tires of the car. You will learn to focus less on English words and word order—to express the idea, not the word.

You're ready to start the first set of practice activities on the road to becoming skilled in American Sign Language. As you progress through this chapter with facial expressions, natural gestures and mimed activities, you should find them quite familiar to you . . . so familiar that you might find yourself thinking "deja vu". . . "I've seen this before."

# Put on a Happy Face

. . . as well as a proud or tired face. You can say a lot with just your face and that's important when you're communicating exclusively with visual information. At the end of subsequent chapters you will see facial expressions appropriate to the subject matter of the chapter.

As you progress through the activities in this book, you can check your growing ability to visualize by "reading" the pictures first and then checking the text. To get you started, look at the extremely happy fellow in the first photograph below. If he translated his facial expression into words, which of these statements would he be making? Match each of the statements in the inside columns with the facial expression that best communicates it. Watch yourself in a mirror to see how well you're able to copy each facial expression.

a

b

c

d

1. I can't move another muscle.
2. That's the best cheesecake I've ever tasted.
3. Kill the umpire!
4. Sometimes you do the strangest things.

Check your impressions against the following: [a. (6); b. (3); c. (8); d. (7); e. (2); f. (9); g. (5); h. (1); i. (4); j. (10)]

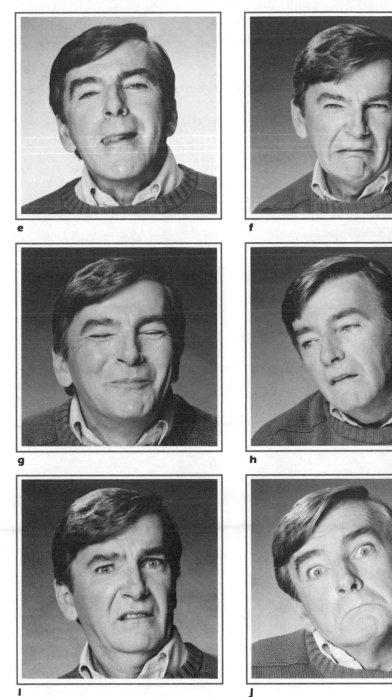

e

f

g

h

i

J

5. Stop before I burst out laughing.
6. I just won a trip to Hawaii!
7. What do you mean we have to make an emergency landing!
8. I accept this award with great pride.
9. That's disgusting!
10. I haven't got the slightest idea where they are.

# Rated PG: Polite Gesturing

You really know a lot about gesturing already. You'll see for yourself when you match each of the statements in the inside columns with the natural gesture that would communicate it. Notice that facial expressions are a part of natural gestures.

Start by looking through all ten of the following photographs. If this person were trying to communicate with you, what do you think he might be saying? Then go through the photographs one by one and match each with the statement we suggest he's trying to communicate. As you "read" the photographs try to stretch your visual receptive skills by thinking of other natural gestures that are not shown here. Provide a related verbal statement for them too. Just remember that this activity is still rated PG.

a

b

c

d

1. I wonder where I left my car keys?

2. We left the fish in the refrigerator too long.

3. Bye! Have a good trip!

4. My daughter is in the second row in the daisy costume.

Check your impressions against the following: [a. (2); b. (1); c. (5); d. (7); e. (8); f. (3); g. (4); h. (6); i. (9); j. (10)]

e

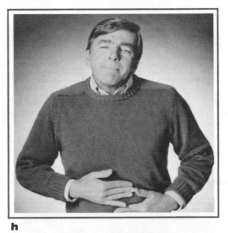

f

g

h

5. I still don't see them anywhere.
6. It must have been something I ate.
7. I think everything will be fine now.
8. The surgery was a complete success!!
9. Don't come any closer.
10. Thanks for all your help.

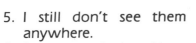

i

j

# Just Like Child's Play

The masters of mime are, of course, Charlie Chaplin and Marcel Marceau. But if you're familiar with the game of charades, you know a lot already about the fundamentals of mime. Mime is just like doing the activity itself—with one significant difference. You must imagine all of the objects used in the activity. . . in this case balls, bats, cue sticks, rods, bows, gloves and oars. By now you should be aware that facial expressions are a part of all the visual information you will be communicating throughout the book.

You'll see just how much you already know by matching each of the following sports with the related action in the inside activity columns that would communicate it. What other activities are you able to communicate simply by miming some recognizable action?

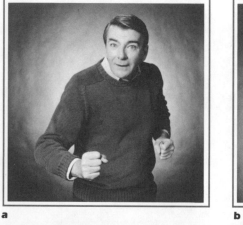

a

b

1. Basketball
2. Billiards
3. Boxing
4. Fishing

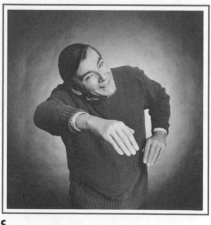

c

d

Check your impressions against the following: [a. (6); b. (1); c. (10); d. (9); e. (5); f. (7); g. (2); h. (8); i. (3); j. (4)]

5. Baseball
6. Running
7. Archery
8. Bowling
9. Canoeing
10. Swimming

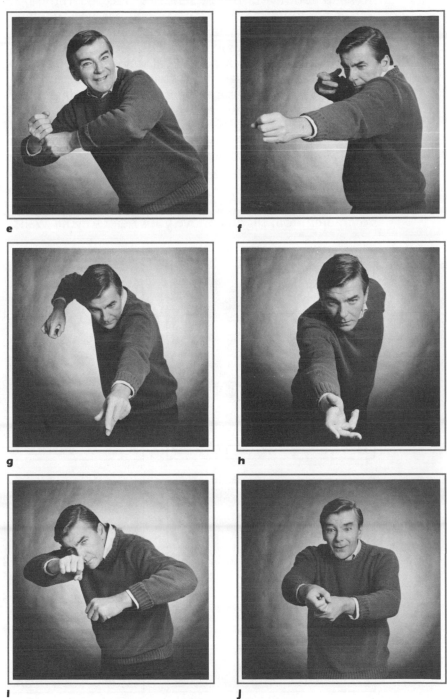

e

f

g

h

i

j

# *Seeing Eye to Eye*

The most effective way to read visual communication is to keep your eyes on the "sender's" face, as in the first set of photographs below. As a beginner, you will tend to follow the sender's hands instead of focusing your attention on the face, as in the second set of photographs. As you gain skill, your peripheral vision will expand to receive all related visual information, as if you were watching an oversize television screen. It will take time to acquire this skill, so have patience.

Practice "sending" and "receiving" the gestures, mime and facial expressions you practiced earlier while keeping your eyes on the sender's face. Practice with a partner or observe yourself in the mirror. As you and your partner take turns sending visual information, limit your gestures to an area from slightly above your head to your waist.

**RIGHT**

**WRONG**

# Meeting Face to Face

Find a partner and take turns sending the information below using natural gestures, mime and facial expressions.

"Hi."

"Nice to meet you."

"How are you?"

"Fine."

"That's good."

"Goodbye."

# NOTES:

Chapter 2

# 2-D or Not 2-D?
Two-Dimensional Lines, Shapes & Patterns

n Chapter Two you will use different combinations of your fingers to draw two-dimensional lines, shapes, patterns and objects in the air. The techniques you are about to learn are some of the conventions for expressing visual-gestural information which are also elements of American Sign Language. They will become the building blocks to make scenes, to show action clearly, and ultimately, to tell stories, which you will learn to do in later chapters.

As you do these activities, you may find them more challenging than you expected because many of the ways you will move your fingers and hands will be unfamiliar to you. Do as many of the activities in this chapter as it takes to make these hand movements as comfortable as natural gestures.

Let us start with "mountain", the idea, not the word. It is easy to express the shape of a "mountain" as a two-dimensional line drawing in the air.

See how the index finger draws the outline of the mountain shape in the air. Compare the hand positions of the photos with the illustrations.

Suppose you now want to express "rainbow." Drawing successive arcs below each other could express a rainbow. But drawing lines all together would be more efficient and the meaning would be clearer.

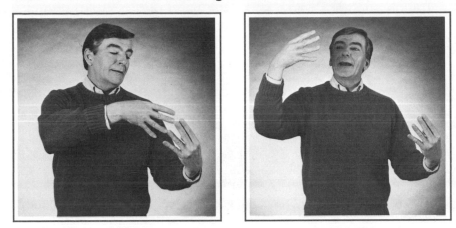

When using the index finger of one hand as if it were a paintbrush drawing in the air, the finger can go in any direction. However, when using more than one finger on one or both hands the hand points up to create vertical lines; sideways to create horizontal lines.

Notice how the hands are held with the palms facing toward you when you draw with more than one finger in a horizontal position. You will learn the conventional ways of expressing patterns that use multiple lines by following the examples in this chapter. You will also learn the accepted ways to show discs, thin lines, parallel lines and symmetrical lines and shapes, as well as the accepted ways of showing patterns of dots, squares, circles and intersecting lines. All of these conventions are based on communicating visual information in the most efficient and clear manner.

Use facial expressions to enhance the meaning of your gestures. Although most of the facial expressions you will find in this book will look familiar to you, you probably have not used facial expressions for concepts like "thin" or "thick" before. Practice adding these meaningful facial expressions to the information you are conveying with your hands and you will become more and more skilled as a visual communicator.

In doing the activities in this chapter, think of the many applications for two-dimensional gesturing. These movements will be useful tools to communicate the shape of a flower or the pattern of a flag.

Practice these exercises until they feel natural. Let your comfort level be your guide. If you think you are reaching beyond that point, be sure to ask yourself whether 2-D or not 2-D?

# Back to the Drawing Board

Become comfortable conveying visual information by drawing lines, shapes and patterns in the air. You can use one, two, three, four or all five fingers as brushes in the space in front of you as a canvas on which you can draw lines, shapes and patterns. The photographs below show the hand position with the palm facing out—for drawing vertical lines. Examine the illustrations accompanying each photograph. Copy each one, using the appropriate hand position.

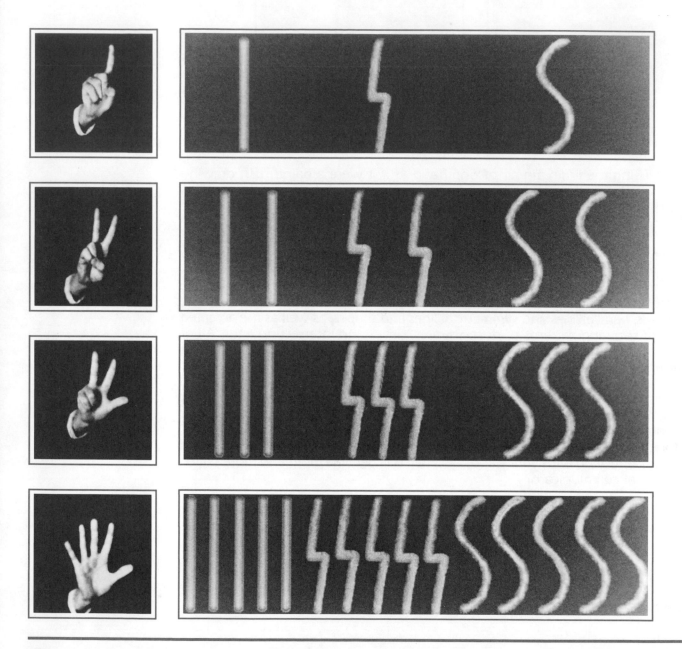

Your creativity would be limited if you were able only to draw vertical lines. When you are using only your index finger, you can draw both vertical and horizontal lines without changing the position of your hand. However, when you are using more than one finger, you must change the position of your hand and face your palm inward to draw horizontal lines. Form each of the hand positions in the photographs below, and create each of the accompanying illustrations.

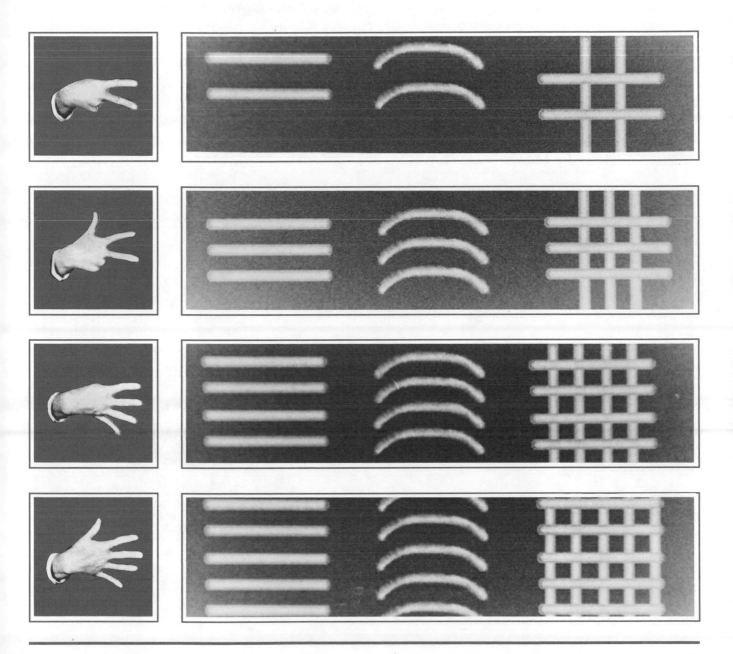

# Jumping in With Both Hands

Read each of the following photographs and copy them, using both hands. You can use both index fingers, as positioned in the first photograph below, to draw both horizontally and vertically without changing the direction of your hands. Using the illustrations as models, practice the horizontal and vertical designs with all the finger groups. When drawing with two, four or five fingers on both hands, remember to face your palms outward for vertical lines and inward, one hand above the other, for horizontal lines. Notice that no designs are practiced using solely the thumbs since that would be too awkward.

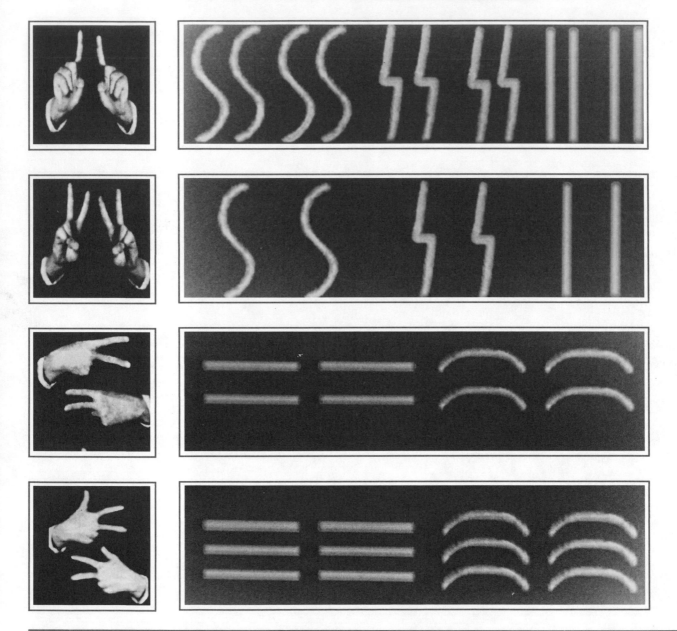

# Making Special Arrangements

Read the photographs below to see how to create disks, thin lines and parallel lines and shapes by using different one and two-handed finger combinations. Curve your fingers to make the rounded shape of the disk. You can use one or both pinkies to show very thin lines. By using the index and middle fingers of one or both hands you can create parallel lines if you keep the same distance between your fingers. You can create lines using the thumb and index finger and move your fingers out and in to create a symmetrical shape like a diamond. To create the trim on a dress, move the hands apart as you repeat the pattern.

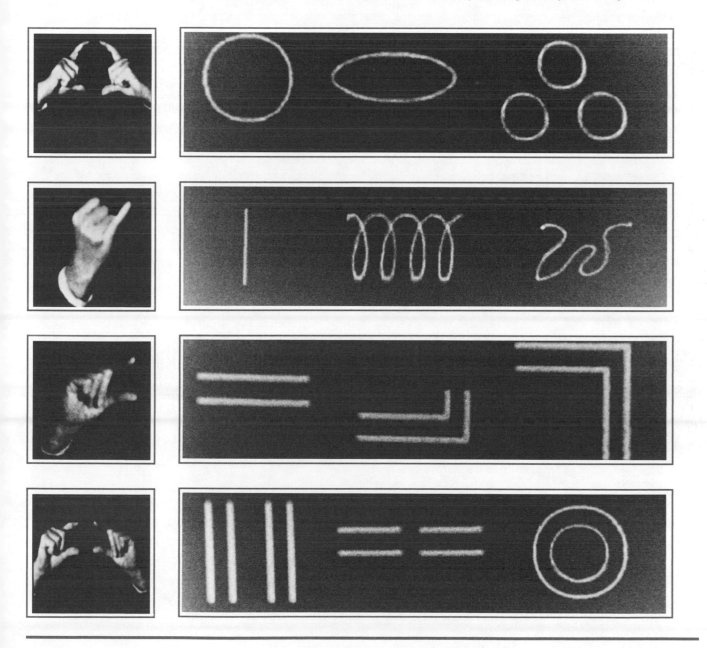

# Creating Your Own Handiwork

You can create dot, square, crossing and circle patterns by using some additional one and two-handed shapes. Start with the dot pattern, the easiest of which is created with a single curved index finger. You can use one or more fingers on one or both hands to create a variety of dotted patterns. You can move the dots you created—one-by-one or two-by-two—vertically or horizontally to show the additional dots in the pattern. If you are creating dots two-by-two, you can also move them outward from the middle to create the additional dots of a column or a row.

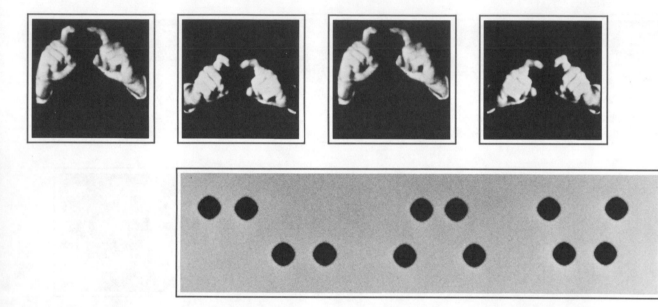

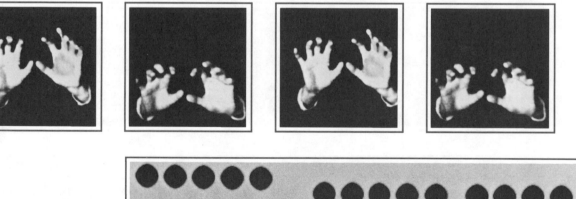

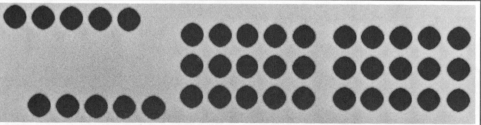

# Putting a Square Peg...

Position the thumb and index finger of one or both hands to create two sides of a square shape. Turn the wrist, keeping palm out, to finish the square. Continue alternating this position of the hands back and forth while moving the hands down, to show all of the squares in a column. Reposition your hand(s) next to the place where you started gesturing your first column to create additional columns. Create intersecting patterns simply by crossing both index fingers and moving the crossing fingers down or across to show any additional parts of the pattern.

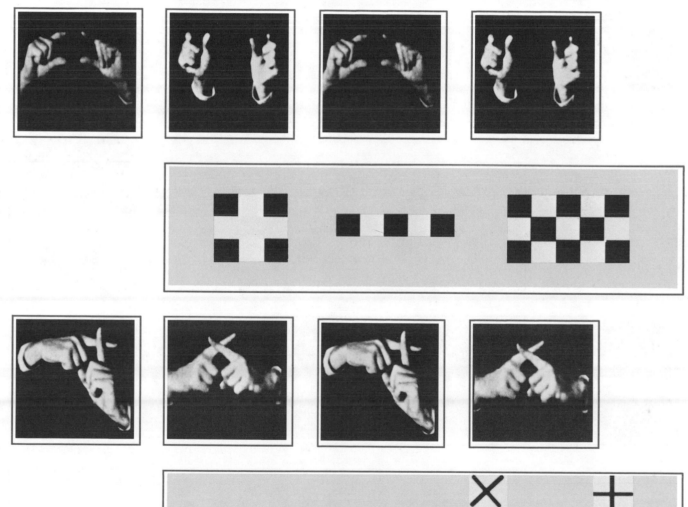

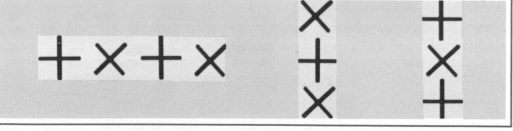

# Into a Round Hole

You can create hole or circle patterns by touching the index finger and thumb of one or both hands to form the round shape and pointing the other fingers upward. You can move the one or two circles you created vertically, horizontally or from the middle outward (for two circles at a time) to show the additional circles in the pattern, one-by-one or two-by-two. If you are forming a circle made of smaller circles you can use one hand to create all the small circles on the perimeter of the larger circle. Or, using both hands, you can create symmetrical sides starting at the top and ending at the bottom of the larger circle.

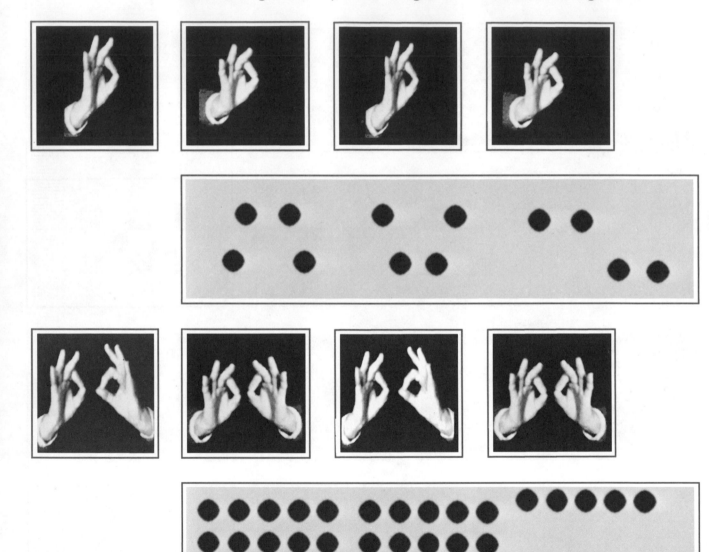

# Written All Over Your Face

Notice the specific meaning that each of the following facial expressions communicates. Then, copy them.

**thin**

**thick**

**soft**

**hard**

**light**

**dark**

Using two-dimensional gestures and facial expressions, express the following:

thin lines

thick symmetrical lines

soft dots

hard zig-zag

light arcs

dark squares

# NOTES:

28

# Chapter 3

# You Are About to Enter Another Dimension

## Three-Dimensional Shapes

ourneying into the third dimension means adding depth and definition to your shapes. You will be amazed to learn how much you can communicate simply by mastering four basic shapes: the ball, cone, cylinder and box. The box can be further broken down into component parts: sides. You can use the front of your hand to represent the front of a side; the back of your hand to represent the back. This distinction is especially important for communicating point-of-view—the way in which something is viewed. The last photograph in the series below, for example, may communicate that you are viewing an interior wall and must be inside, not outside, a room.

Let the shape of your hands suggest the shape of the object. Keep your fingers straight for the box shape as in the first photograph below. Curve your fingers for the ball, cone and cylinder shapes. The second photograph below might be the base of a cone or part of a large cylinder.

Whatever shape you are gesturing, be sure to leave enough space with your hands to accommodate its size: small, medium or large.

Whether gesturing a ball, cone, cylinder or box, let the position of your hands indicate the orientation of the object. A medium-sized cylinder, as in the photographs below, would be held with both hands side by side to indicate a horizontal orientation, one hand over the other for a vertical orientation.

The techniques you learned in Chapter Two for creating two-dimensional lines, shapes, patterns and objects can be integrated into the gesturing of three-dimensional shapes. For example, the meaning of a three-dimensional object can be enhanced by two-dimensional details; the important paper you are looking for is in a box with a checkerboard cover. Or perhaps you want to express a cone-shaped lampshade with a border at its base as in the photographs below. Notice that first the three-dimensional shape, the cone, is gestured, then the two-dimensional detail is applied.

Imagine, if you will, a destination where you hold the power to create shapes with depth, where the skills you develop now will enhance your signed communication later. Be prepared, for you are about to enter another dimension.

# The Ball Shape: A Round When You Need It

Of all the basic shapes you will gesture, none will be easier or more obvious than the ball. Creating the shape is as easy as imitating the shape with your hands. Adjust the distance between your hands to show the size of the ball while maintaining the curved shape with your fingers. You may use one hand for gesturing half a ball: a dome.

The cone shape is almost as simple as the ball shape to gesture. However, to show its complete shape you will need to move your hands from its point while increasing the distance between your hands until you reach its base. You can always adjust the direction of the movement if the cone happens to be in a horizontal position. For a variation of the cone shape, begin at the base and create a curved cone that you might use later to gesture elephant's tusks or a cornucopia.

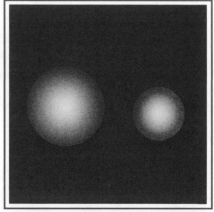

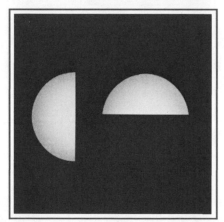

Gesture the illustrations and the following shapes:

a large ball with a thick line around the middle

a medium-sized ball with dots all over it

one large, one medium, and one small ball in a row

one large, one medium, and one small ball in a vertical column

two domes, both facing up one dome facing up, and one facing down

# The Cone Shape: Coming to the Point

Read the photographs below showing the hand position for gesturing the cone shape and gesture the illustration.

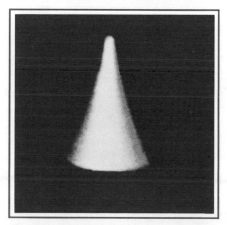

Gesture the illustrations and other cones:

a miniature cone

a short, wide cone

a tall, thin cone

a short, thin cone

all of the above in an inverted position

# The Cylinder Shape: Just a Rod With Class

There are three different hand positions for gesturing cylinders. The position you use depends on the size of the cylinder you wish to gesture: small, medium or large. Touch your thumb and index finger on both hands and extend all of your other fingers to show a small cylinder. Extend both hands out from the center to show its length as in the photographs below. You will change the direction of your hand movement to up and down if the cylinder is in a vertical position. Practice gesturing the small cylinders in the accompanying illustrations.

Hold your hands in semi-circles to show the shape of a medium-sized cylinder and place them in a side-by-side position, as in the first two photographs on the opposite page. Hold one hand over the other to show a vertical position.

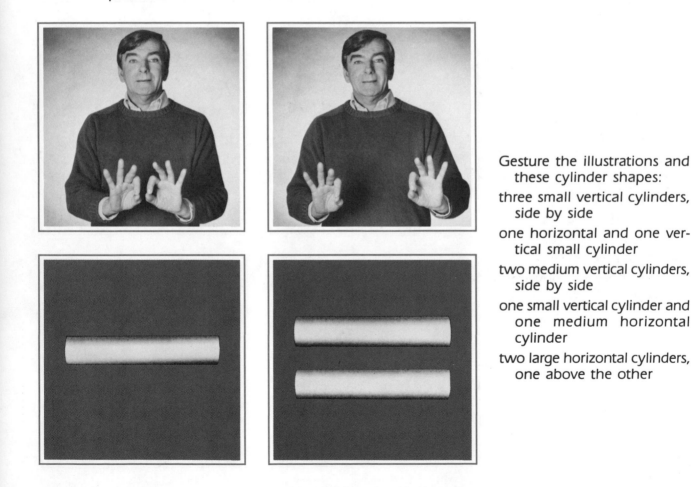

Gesture the illustrations and these cylinder shapes:

three small vertical cylinders, side by side

one horizontal and one vertical small cylinder

two medium vertical cylinders, side by side

one small vertical cylinder and one medium horizontal cylinder

two large horizontal cylinders, one above the other

Position your hands to face each other to show a large-sized cylinder as in the remaining photographs.

Try these too:

three large vertical cylinders, side by side

one large vertical cylinder and one medium vertical cylinder above it

one small vertical cylinder and one large horizontal cylinder, side by side

one large horizontal cylinder and one large vertical cylinder side by side

# The Box Shape: Side by Side by Side by Side

It should come as no surprise to you that you will straighten the position of your hands to form the box shape. You will reposition your hands to form the front and back sides as in the first photograph below, and then its two sides.

The box shape is a useful gesturing tool and one side of the box can be used alone. As seen in the first photograph on the opposite page, facing your palm forward represents the interior view of a flat service—the interior side of a door. Showing the back of your hand can represent an exterior view of the same door. If you create a four-sided box and wish to add a top and bottom to it, one hand with the palm facing up can represent the bottom of the box's interior. One hand with the palm facing down can represent its top, as viewed from the top.

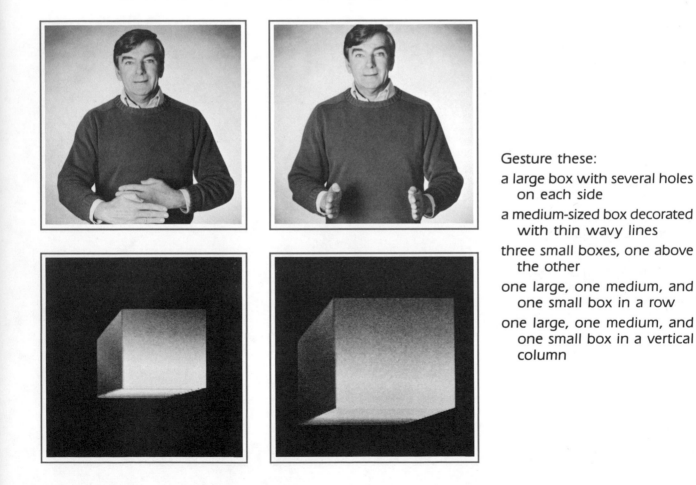

Gesture these:

a large box with several holes on each side

a medium-sized box decorated with thin wavy lines

three small boxes, one above the other

one large, one medium, and one small box in a row

one large, one medium, and one small box in a vertical column

Face palm outward to show a box's lid viewed from the front; show the back of your hand for the back view. Two hands touching show the interior back of a box.

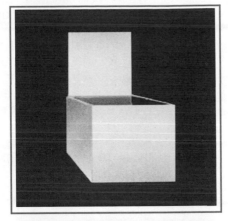

Gesture the illustrations and these views:

an interior view with your fingers extended upward

an exterior view with your fingers extended upward

an interior view with your fingers extended sideways

an exterior view with your fingers extended sideways

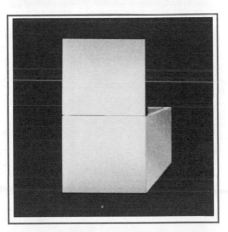

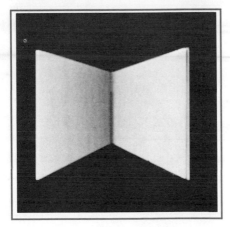

# Rules Governing the Board

You may often find it necessary to gesture two attached boards in different positions. For example, you may wish to show a slanted roof, a corner of a room, a straight-backed chair, or an open door or window. To prepare yourself to create any one of these objects you would need to determine the positions of the two boards and decide whether or not both boards were interior views (like two interior walls of a house); both boards were exterior views (like a roof viewed from above); or one was an interior view and the other an exterior view. Then, you would place your hands in the appropriate position to represent the two boards. The first photograph below shows palms out to form two attached boards, palms in, to form an interior point-of-view; the second photograph shows two boards slanting to form a roof.

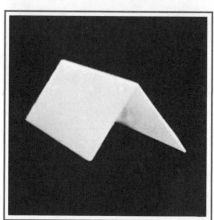

Gesture these using interior and exterior boards:

a roof viewed from above

an interior corner of a room

the exterior corner of a house

the exterior view of a window and window sill

the interior back and side walls of a room

an exterior section of fence, with the interior side of the gate swung open

The photographs below show the hand positions for very narrow and very thick boards. Gesture the illustrations.

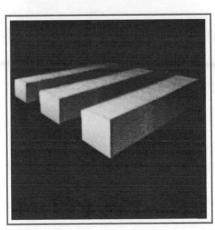

Now try these:

two narrow boards side by side

three narrow boards in a row

two thick boards side by side

four thick boards on top of each other

alternating narrow and thick boards in a row

a fence made of alternating narrow and thick vertical boards

# A New Dimension to Modern Art

t's a bird. It's a plane. Actually, we don't know what it is, but we do know that it is created from balls, cones, cylinders and boxes. You can combine these basic three-dimensional shapes to make unusual objects. The practice that you get here will enable you to gesture real objects in the next chapter and soon after use them in action. While the practice may seem bizarre, the absence of a verbal definition to this object of art will help you to continue to think visually.

Observe how to create the unusual object seen in the first illustration by combining the three-dimensional shapes you've already practiced. It begins with the box shape. . . all four sides. It has a covering on it, perhaps a roof, made of four boards that taper off and connect at a top point. A ball is balancing itself on top of that point and a small cylinder extends up from the ball.

# Searching for a Deeper Meaning

You can use the following facial expressions to add meaning to the three-dimensional shapes you created.

small

large

strange

fascinating

Gesture and include facial expressions to create the following:

small cylinder

large box

strange bottle

fascinating pearl

heavy ball

light

heavy

**NOTES:**

42

Chapter 4
# Taking Matters Into Your Own Hands
Three-Dimensional Objects

ongratulations! You have reached a milestone in your learning. You should now be able to express visually any three-dimensional object that is derived from one or more of the four basic shapes you practiced in Chapter Three: the ball, cone, cylinder and box.

You can create most concrete objects by applying the techniques for making basic three-dimensional shapes. You can enhance the meaning of those basic shapes with two-dimensional detail, as well as with facial expressions. Use this chapter to consolidate what you know and to strengthen your ability to think in pictures. This will prepare you for your next leap forward in Chapter Five, when you will put various three-dimensional objects in scenes.

The first object you will gesture is a walking cane. Start by picturing the walking cane in your mind. Can you identify its basic shape? Yes, it's a cylinder. Are there any other basic shapes in the walking cane? No, just the cylinder. So, now you know what shape you will gesture, but what size cylinder will you be gesturing: small, medium or large sized?

The medium-sized cylinder seems to be the appropriate shape for a respectable walking cane. Now, one more decision before you gesture the object. Which gesturing strategy will work best: top to bottom or bottom to top; left to right to left? Center to perimeter or perimeter to center? The top-to-bottom strategy should work well for gesturing the walking cane.

Now that you have a clear picture in your mind of the object you're going to gesture, identified its component shapes, determined its relative size; and decided on a gesturing strategy, all that's left is to gesture the walking cane.

Begin by placing your hands close together at the top end of the walking cane. Keep the bottom hand in this position while the top hand creates the shape and length of the cane. Move your hand to gesture its shape and its relative length and...Voila! A walking cane!

The last photograph of the sequence above shows the actual object that was gestured. This photograph shows you how we pictured the object since sometimes people do picture objects differently. By showing you the actual object you will understand how the various components contribute to the complete gestured object.

Are you ready to transform gestured shapes into objects by taking matters into your own hands?

# The Ball Shape: Takes Your Breath Away

Observe how to gesture a balloon. Notice how the size of the ball shape expands to show the balloon becoming larger and larger while the hands stay in the same curved position.

If you create a large ball and add two-dimensional detail outlining the continents, the ball shape becomes planet Earth.

To gesture a snowman, stack a large, medium and small ball on top of each other. Add some two-dimensional detail to show its face, perhaps a cone to show its nose. By adding three holes to a large ball, it becomes a bowling ball. The meaning of the ball shape will be conveyed by action, facial expression and surface details.

Gesture:

marbles
a clown's nose
a pearl
a ball of yarn
a basketball
a crystal ball
a hot air balloon
a cantaloupe
a snowball
the sun and planets

# The Box Shape: Jewel of a Container

Observe how to gesture a jewelry box. Notice how the size and top of the box are all created in their appropriate places to give an accurate presentation of the box. Gesture a square cuff link and the use for the box becomes clear.

The size of any box is an important clue to what you are gesturing. By gesturing a small rectangular box you can make a brick. A large, rectangular box becomes a packing crate. A small, square box can be a simple gift box with some two-dimensional detail added to show the design of the wrapping paper.

Use the box shape as a starting point to gesture the objects listed in the activity column. Don't limit yourself to this list.

Gesture:

a milk carton
dresser drawers
an automatic camera
a washing machine
a grandfather's clock
a tissue box
an upright piano
a television set
a water fountain
a toaster

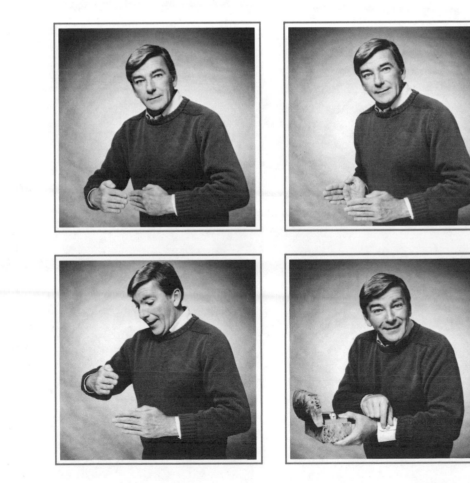

# The Cylinder Shape: Rolling In Dough

Observe how to gesture a rolling pin. Notice how the hand shape changes as the size of the cylinder changes from medium to small. The hand shape is an important clue in communicating the size of the cylindrical objects.

Think how your hand shapes would change as you gesture an elongated, large cylinder and add some small perpendicular projections for climbing on to show a telephone pole. Create a three-foot, medium cylinder that tapers from the top to the bottom to form a baseball bat. Make a short, small cylinder and add some two-dimensional holes down its length to create a clarinet. Gesture a short medium-sized cylinder for a microphone, attaching it to a long, thin cylinder if it's on a stand. Gesture the rolling pin and each of the objects using the cylinder shape.

Gesture:

an ear of corn
a cue stick
a garden hose
a barbershop pole
a candlestick
an aerosol can
a flashlight
a bottle
a telescope
a drum and drumsticks

# The Cone Shape: Life of the Party

Observe how to gesture a party hat. This party hat seems to require a medium-sized cone. Once the cone shape is formed, notice how the size and shape of the base of the cone is maintained as it is moved to the head.

The cone is the main gestural feature of such objects as a funnel, a watercooler cup, a megaphone, a pine tree and a party hat. Gesture a small cone to create a funnel and an even smaller cone shape to make a watercooler cup. Form a medium cone to show a megaphone. Gesture a very large cone to create a pine tree. Now, gesture the party hat and each of these objects using the cone shape. What other objects could you gesture using the cone shape? Gesture them as well as the objects in the activity column.

Gesture:

a volcano
elephant tusks
a traffic cone
a pine cone
a vase
a pastry funnel
a teepee
a stalactite
a lamp shade
a carrot

# Looks Good Enough to Eat

Food comes in all shapes and sizes. You've already practiced making a round cantaloupe with a medium-sized ball shape; a rectangular carton of milk using a small box shape; a long, cylindrical ear of corn by forming a medium-sized, short cylinder; and a carrot using a small cone shape.

Now, observe below how to gesture an ice cream cone by creating a small cone shape and topping it with a ball-shaped scoop of ice cream. Notice how each of the pieces of this visual treat is gestured in its appropriate place to communicate "ice cream cone." First, one hand moves up slightly to create the cone shape since the larger end is at the top. Then, the hand forming the top of the cone remains in place as the scoop of ice cream is added.

Gesture:

a banana

an apple

a sandwich

a bunch of grapes

a stalk of celery

a pumpkin

a slice of watermelon

a chicken leg

a strand of spaghetti

a hotdog in bun

# In All Shapes and Sizes

Most objects are made up of more than one shape. A table, for example, is gestured using the box shape and usually four cylinder shapes; a Christmas tree with decorative ornaments is gestured using a large cone shape and traditionally many ornamental balls; and a skateboard is gestured using a rectangular-shaped box and ball shapes for wheels. Observe how to gesture a decorated Christmas tree. Notice how the appropriate sized cone is gestured first to create the tree. The ornaments are then added to its branches.

What other objects could you gesture using more than one three-dimensional shape? Gesture them as well as the objects in the activity column. Try to add two-dimensional detail to the objects you gesture whenever possible.

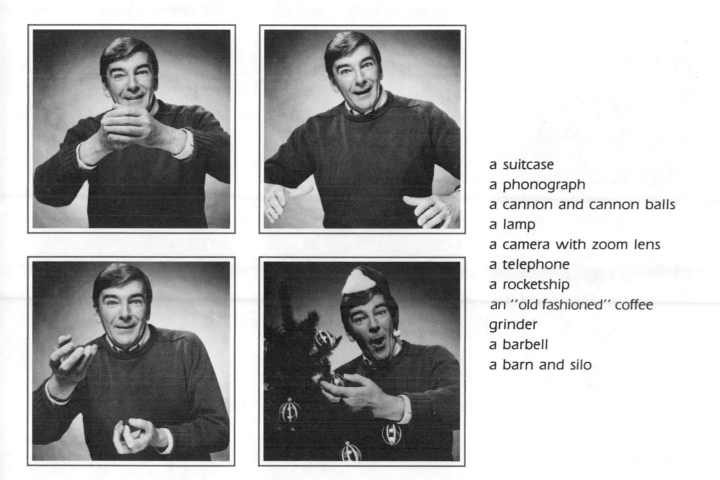

a suitcase

a phonograph

a cannon and cannon balls

a lamp

a camera with zoom lens

a telephone

a rocketship

an "old fashioned" coffee grinder

a barbell

a barn and silo

# A Change for the Better

Create an object that has one of the basic shapes: ball, box, cylinder or cone. Then, think of another object with the same basic shape and change the first object into the new one. To get started, observe how to gesture a baseball bat and change it into a flashlight. Observe how the long cylinder of a baseball bat must be pressed down to become the small cylinder of a flashlight.

To communicate the concepts more clearly, notice that the bat was held in a batting stance and the light was gestured coming from the flashlight. Gesture a bat and transform it into a flashlight. Then, transform the flashlight into a fishing pole, the pole into a pencil, the pencil into a thermometer. Begin with a newly gestured object whenever you wish.

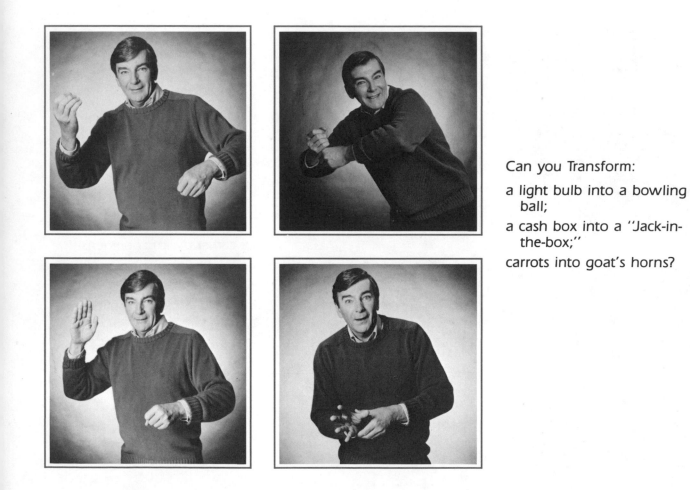

Can you Transform:

a light bulb into a bowling ball;

a cash box into a "Jack-in-the-box;"

carrots into goat's horns?

# Just One Look...

can add meaning to any of the three-dimensional objects you gesture. Copy and use the facial expressions below.

**fragile**

**sturdy**

**delicious**

**bitter**

**expensive**

**cheap**

Express the following:
a "fragile" vase
a "sturdy" washing machine
a "delicious" chicken leg
some "bitter" grapes
an "expensive" strand of
    pearls
some "cheap" crates

# NOTES:

Chapter 5
# The Right Place at the Right Time
## Placement of Objects

reating a scene, such as a room, is similar to creating an object. You must determine all the component parts and gesture them in their proper places. To keep your gesturing field uncluttered and free of confusing elements you must learn to avoid making unnecessary movements as you gesture. This means deliberately repositioning your hands each time you move them to a new location. This will help you to avoid stacking objects, one on top of the other.

If you gesture a clock with hands, for example, be sure to place them on the clock's face.

If you want to show all the detail of an object, such as a door, you include the door knob in the proper place. Notice in the first photograph below that the complete door is gestured first to establish the identity of the object. Then, the door knob is placed on the door.

Later, you will create a room, its component parts and the objects within the room, including a clock, and put them all in their proper places in the scene.

As you gesture a scene, you will want to make your creation visually consistent. If you were gesturing a room, for example, you would want to show the ceiling above the floor and the light fixture hanging from the ceiling.

As the angle at which a scene is observed changes, so does the way in which the objects in the scene are gestured. If you look straight ahead at a house, the front door will probably be facing you as in the first photograph below. However, if you change your position in relation to the house, you also change your position in relation to the front door. Consequently, the placement of the door, as in the pictures below, changes as the position from whch it is viewed changes.

A skillful visual communicator will also consider perspective when gesturing a scene. For example, the shape of an object, such as a road, will appear to taper off into the background and finally converge at a point.

Give yourself ample time to practice and develop skills in placement. In short, make sure that everything is gestured in the right place at the right time.

# A Place for Everything

It is now time to combine the gestures for several objects to create a very simple scene. Observe how to gesture the basic parts of a room. Notice first how the palms face out to represent interior walls as the hands create the basic shape and size of the room in the photographs below.

The photographs on the opposite page shows how each part is added to the room, in its appropriate relationship to the walls. The first set of two photographs shows the floor, the second shows the window and the third set shows the door. The floor is logically placed at the base of the walls you have created, indicating the area of the room. A window is inserted into the wall to the left, and a door to the right, so each has a distinct position.

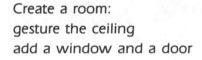

Create a room:
gesture the ceiling
add a window and a door

Notice how the concept of window and door are more clearly communicated by showing how each opens.

Modify the room:

add a window to another wall

reverse the new window with the door

# Everything in its Place

Now add objects to the room you just created. Be sure to put each object in this scene in its proper place . . . not stacked on top of each other.

Observe how to gesture a table with a lamp and clock placed on it. Notice how the backs of the hands are used to represent the top, or exterior, of the table in the photographs below. Add the lamp and clock to the scene, as in the photographs on the opposite page. Each object is placed on the table top that was just created. The base, neck, shade and bulb of the lamp are gestured first with each part in its proper place to avoid stacking. Notice how one hand maintains the shape of the lampshade while the other lights the bulb. Notice also how the hands are placed within the clock's frame right where they belong.

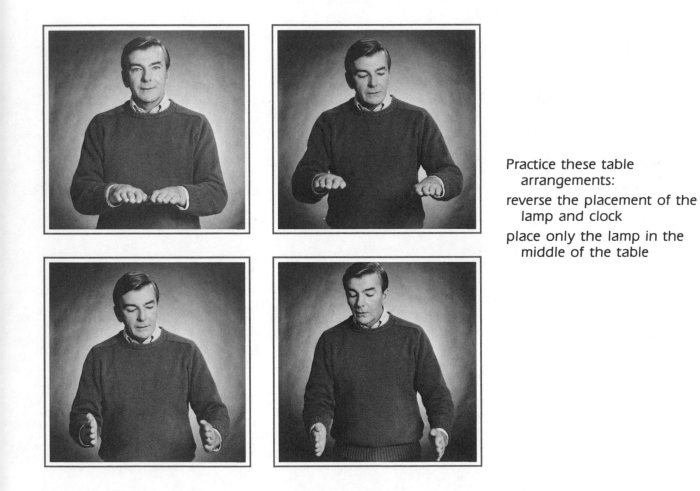

Practice these table arrangements:

reverse the placement of the lamp and clock

place only the lamp in the middle of the table

The last two photographs show how the clock is gestured on the side of the table that is empty of other objects.

Make more table
  arrangements:
substitute a vase for the lamp
add a vase and place it
  between the lamp and clock

# Making A Scene

Create complex scenes by using the same technique of gesturing each part of the scene in the right place. Observe how to gesture the exterior of a house: roof, sides, and door. In the bottom photographs notice how one hand maintains the position of the roof while the other places the door and then the sky into the scene in their appropriate places in relation to the roof.

How would you gesture a monument such as the Lincoln Memorial—with its slanted roof, broad steps leading upward, bordered by thick walls, and pillars along its entire length? Consider a long rectangular covered bridge with a water wheel on one side and a river flowing past. How would you gesture this? Or picture a house on a cliff along a rugged seacoast with a lighthouse attached to the house. Try to gesture each of these scenes.

Create these scenes:

the courtyard of a Russian church with three onion domes

a windmill with large blades on a flat field

a two-story house with a long porch

# Considering All the Angles

From the sequence for house observe how one piece, the roof, is gestured to show different viewing angles.

Gesture each from varying angles:

table: viewed from below; viewed from straight ahead

stairs: viewed from straight ahead; viewed from the side

suspension bridge: viewed from the side; viewed as if walking across

# Gaining a New Perspective

Objects look closer together as they taper off into the horizon like the sides of a road in the first two photographs below. In the second set of photographs below a row of trees is being gestured. Notice how the apparent size of objects changes with perspective.

How would you communicate the perspective in a scene of a long hallway with many open doors along one wall and a row of ceiling lights down the entire length of the hallway? Try to gesture the Great Wall of China stretching into the distance over hilly land. A building is on top of a hill in the distance alongside the wall with a long winding walkway up to the building. Or picture a long, massive pipe extending forward along flat ground with a person standing inside the pipe at its far end.

Create these scenes in perspective:

hilly land; endless road stretching into distance; broken line down middle of road

railroad platform; two sets of parallel tracks stretching into the distance; bridge across tracks

long, narrow pipes in stacks to right and left; person between stacks at far end, standing

# Taking a Good Look Around

You can use the following facial expressions to add meaning to any of the objects within the scenes you gesture.

clean

dirty

Express the following:

"clean" desk
"dirty" desk
"plain" room
"elegant" room
"cheerful" room
"gloomy" room

plain

elegant

cheerful

gloomy

# NOTES:

Chapter 6
# Lights! Camera! Action!
## Showing Objects and People in Action

n Chapter Six you will discover, as you did with the activities in Chapter One, that you already have experience communicating action without spoken words. Mime is only one step away from doing the real action. Imagine yourself in the real situation of driving a car. One action you do is turn the steering wheel. Now come back to reality. Do the same action of steering, but without the steering wheel—or the car for that matter. You can see that acting something out can be as natural as doing the real action itself.

An action can take place in many different contexts. The action of writing, for example, requires a writing implement such as a pencil, pen or chalk. If you were writing on surfaces of similar size in similar locations, the action of using any of these writing implements would look about the same. However, if you were scribbling notes on a small pad in your hand, signing an autograph, or writing on a blackboard, the actions would look quite different.

It is important to add the right facial expression and body language to your action so that the clearest meaning possible may be communicated.

Is the man secretively writing on his pad some sort of spy? The next man appears pleased to provide his autograph. Is the man writing on the blackboard concentrating on a mathematical equation?

Often, to communicate an action clearly, you must first gesture the objects you will use. For example, did you notice when the man signs his autograph, he gestures the book, photo, or program on which he is writing. Observe in the following example how the batter creates his bat before approaching the plate.

You can modify the meaning of your communication by the intensity and speed with which you communicate. Suppose your car breaks down and you want to write a letter of complaint. How would you gesture that quality of writing? Which of these photographs best communicates your level of intensity?

You've learned to create your props and set your scenes. So ready on the set—lights, camera, action!

# Staying in Shape

You've already had practice creating all kinds of objects. Now it's time to do something with them. So let's get back to basics by creating the four basic shapes: ball, cone, cylinder and box.

Start by making a cylinder. Make it a medium-sized one as in the photographs below. Move it from a vertical to a horizontal position. Raise it. Then move it back to a vertical position and point it outward. Make a circle with it. Make it zigzag. Throw it up in the air and catch it before it crashes to the ground. Be sure to maintain the same size and shape for the cylinder as you move it about. For variety you might want to change the size of the cylinder or any of the other basic shapes you practice with.

Shape up with these shapes, too:

a ball

a box

a cone

# Easier Done Than Said

Communicating actions can be as simple as doing the action itself as with eat, drink, carry, climb, push, and pull.

Act out the following simple actions:

| | |
|---|---|
| eat | cook |
| drink | open |
| carry | close |
| climb | draw |
| push | buy |
| pull | wash |
| count | laugh |
| paint | drop |
| dig | pick up |
| smell | throw |
| shout | sew |
| write | sleep |

# I See What You Mean

You can include more information to communicate an activity clearly. Shoving an imagined pan into an imagined oven might communicate "bake", for example, but acting out more of the steps involved and gesturing the pan, the oven and more of the utensils might clear up any confusion. To show "grow" more completely, you might begin by planting the seed and watering it before the plant actually grows—as in the photographs below.

The better you visualize the objects you are gesturing, the more vividly you will communicate them. For example, when you "wrote", "ate", and "washed" in the previous activity, did you wonder whether you were writing while sitting at a table or standing at the blackboard? Were you eating soup or biting into a watermelon? Were you washing your face or your car?

Show exactly what you mean:

cook pancakes
make ice cubes
get ready for bed
pump gas
mow a lawn
buy a candy bar
walk the dog
change a diaper
take a photograph

# Clearing Up Any Confusion

Gestures for "paint" vary as the object changes from a wall to a portrait, a car, fingernails and lips.

Mean exactly what you show:

writing (at a table, on the blackboard)

eating (soup, watermelon, ice cream cone

washing (your face, a car, the dog)

carrying (a suitcase, a carton, a baby)

pushing (a car, a person, a shopping cart)

# Food for Thought

You already practiced gesturing some foods in Chapter Four. However, communicating other foods through gestures may take a little extra thought. "Spaghetti," for example, will require more creativity than communicating "banana" as in the top photos below.

The second pair of photographs shows how you might communicate the wine you drink to wash down the spaghetti. Pulling the cork from the wine bottle before drinking the glass of wine and showing a little of its effects after drinking it might communicate this food concept even more clearly. Thinking beyond the singular word is required. Allow your thought processes to broadly explore the concept related to each food. If you are having a sandwich, are you at a picnic or a cafeteria?

Be creative communicating the following:

eggs, toast, coffee

tuna sandwich, soft drink

apple pie a la mode

steak, mashed potatoes, spinach

taco, beer

birthday cake, punch

# Developing a Green Thumb

Creatively communicate a food like "onion" by showing it grown, pulled up, then prepared for cooking.

Similarly show the life cycle of the following:

corn

potato

banana

tomato

grapefruit

fish

# With a Mind of Its Own

Objects as well as people can be involved in actions as you have already seen when the cylinder you threw into the air in the first activity fell down toward the ground; when the strand of spaghetti moved from the plate and disappeared in the diner's mouth; and when the onion grew. Although inanimate objects don't move under their own power, they may be moved by people or by the forces of nature.

Some other examples are plates that are dropped and break, a flag waves in the wind, water drips from a leaky faucet, a flower grows up from the ground, and a ferris wheel that turns. Observe the photographs showing one object, perhaps a glass bowl, moving as a result of a person's action, and a flag waving in the wind, the result of a force of nature.

Animate these inanimate objects:

- a ball bouncing
- a traffic cone tipping over
- a glass falling off the edge of a table
- a plate breaking in two pieces
- a pendulum swinging
- a drill bit turning
- a raft rising and falling with the waves
- jello shaking

# Actions Speak Louder Than Words...

But not necessarily louder than facial expressions. Notice the specific meaning for each one, then copy them.

**happily**

**sadly**

**energetically**

**wearily**

Express the following:
"happily" cook pancakes
"sadly" dig
"energetically" mow the lawn
"wearily" wash clothes
"confidently" write
"timidly" climb

**confidently**

**timidly**

# NOTES:

**D**id the exertion in Chapter Six take a lot out of you? Standing on center stage to act out every bit of action can be tiring, and not always the most efficient way to communicate actions visually. Representing people with different hand and finger configurations is a convenient way to communicate their action. You can use your index finger to represent the whole person, as in the first photograph below. Or you can represent just the head and torso, as in the second photograph; just the feet, as in the last photograph; or just the legs, as in the first photograph on the opposite page, expressing "stand".

As you did in Chapter Six, remember to consider the objects involved and their location. If you have gestured a house and want a person to walk to it or away from it, make sure your fingers are traveling in the right direction. Observe in the photographs below how hand shapes can also represent actions of the eyes.

Here the hands positioned near the eyes change shape to indicate surprise as the eyes open wide. You can also use hand shapes and finger configurations to show such actions and reactions as watching, reading and showing shock.

One hand shape or finger configuration may be used in different ways. Pointing the index and middle fingers downward, for example, can represent legs standing. Extending them forward in front of your face represents eyes seeing.

You may also use your own face and body as part of your artistic canvas to create the facial features and clothing of the people you gesture. To indicate that Pinocchio's nose got longer when he lied, you may gesture your own nose growing longer. To indicate a lady's sunbonnet, you can gesture placing the bonnet on your own head and tying the ribbon below the chin.

Using hand shapes and finger configurations will also allow you to easily do some activities that are dangerous or difficult, or awkward—such as falling, sliding, diving or crossing your legs. Another benefit is that you are able to communicate more information in a reduced amount of space in front of your body.

Later, you will use hand shapes for gesturing animals and birds. They will free you from miming all the action and instead, let your fingers do the talking.

# A Helping Hand

As your own torso can represent another person's torso, so can your fist and arm be used to represent a person's head and torso. Your index finger can represent a person from head to toe. The photographs below show how to gesture "walk" using these techniques. You can use your index and middle fingers to represent a person from waist to toe, both index fingers to represent a person's legs, and both hands to represent a person's feet, (see opposite page.)

Which technique you use depends on what action you are communicating. For example, if you want to communicate "walk" you'd better represent legs or feet. On the other hand, if you want to communicate a "nod" then you'll definitely need to represent a head. As you will see shortly, you can use many of these representations to show the same action.

Gesture:

Act out: swim, bow, dive, nod

Arm/fist: bow, shake head, jump, fall

Index: fall, jump, ascend, descend

All the above: walk, stand, run, sway, turn around, dance

# On Your Own Two Feet

Observe three more ways to gesture "walk" just by putting one finger or hand in front of the other.

Gesture:

Index/middle: sit, kneel, fall, get up

Index/index: cross legs, limp, hurdle, jump

Hands: tap foot, click heels, stand pigeon-toed, tiptoe

All the above: walk, stand, run, slip, kick, dance

# Let Me Count the Ways

You've seen that you can communicate the same action by using a variety of hand shapes and finger configurations. You can act out "walk", for example, using your own torso. Or, you can use the other techniques you've practiced to show "walk". The photographs below give a sample of the variety of techniques you can apply.

Don't overgeneralize, however, since not all actions provide this versatility. Only one hand shape, the fist, can communicate "bow" and you can represent someone standing on his or her tiptoes only by using both hands. This time, gesture the actions listed in the activity column using all of the ways you've practiced. Think about how the visual picture you are sending might change as you switch from one configuration to another.

Gesture these actions:

walk
run
ascend
descend
jump
trip
fall
stand
turn
dance

# Can't Stand Still

Combine two or more movements. Observe how to gesture the action series lie down, sit, get up and jump.

Try these action series:

skate, fall, get up
stand, sit, cross legs
run, hurdle, run
march, click heels, bow
ascend, look around, sit
ascend, nod, dive
hop, skip, jump
walk, dance, trip
run, walk, sit
ascend, shake head, descend

# Right Before Your Eyes

Use the index finger of one hand to show a person "seeing from" one eye. Now use the index and middle fingers of one hand to show a person "seeing from" both eyes. Notice how the fingers change direction to show a person "looking from" both eyes, as in the third photograph in the series below.

You can also use the thumbs and index fingers of both hands to show eye expressions, as in the final photograph on this page and the first three photographs on the opposite page. Closing the thumbs and index fingers so they touch and extending the other fingers creates eyeballs looking around. Positioning the thumbs and index fingers into semicircles creates widened eyes, such as when we experience shock. Flattening out the thumbs and index fingers indicated eyes squinting. Extending them creates surprise.

See if you can do these:

see
look
look around
search
peek
stare

Also, we show two people "seeing from" both eyes, "looking from" both eyes, and many people "looking out".

See if you can do these too:

recognize
show shock
show surprise
look at each other
squint
close eyes

# When All Is Seen and Done

Now that you have practiced using various hand shapes and finger configurations to represent people in action as well as their eye and facial expressions, you are ready to put them together.

Observe how to gesture the action series of turn around, inspect and show shock. You can use various representations to show "turn around", including the index finger. The fist, however, is most appropriate in this case because the action that follows involves seeing. Therefore, turning the head and torso around is most logical. Once the head is turned, the hand shape changes into two eyes looking around: "inspect." This inspection must have turned up something unexpected, because the eyes open wide to express shock—which is reinforced by the accompanying facial expression.

Put together these actions:

search for someone, walk, dance

ascend, close eyes, dive

look at each other, squint, run

stand, look at each other, click heels

run, jump, look back

sit, cross legs, look around, show surprise

# I Haven't a Thing to Wear

But you can imagine any piece of clothing you desire. Observe how to wear this pullover sweater and hat.

Make a man and woman with these clothes:

a man's...

pants and belt
shirt and tie
watch
socks
shoes

a woman's...

skirt and sash
blouse
necklace
hose
shoes

# I Never Forget a Face

As good as your gesturing has been, something is still missing: facial features. Now it's time to include gestural information about facial features such as face shapes, hair types, eye shapes, eyebrows, noses, mouths, and teeth. You can use two- and three-dimensional gestures to create the enormous variety of facial features of the diverse people we encounter on our planet. Observe how to gesture a straight and a hooked nose in the photographs below. Combine that nose with other facial features and you have a lot of the visual information to distinguish a young Irish girl from an old Middle Eastern man.

Using your own face as the canvas, you can be as brief or as elaborate as you want in adding facial features. The important consideration is to provide the viewer with the information that is necessary for clear communication.

Create a:

man with curly hair, wide eyes, glasses, hooked nose, mustache, holding cigar

man with a covered head, head band, almond-shaped eyes, thin, long eyebrows, thin lips

clown with round face, bald down middle, bushy hair on sides, painted, crescent eyebrows, round nose, big smile

Gesturing a round face, bushy hair, protruding ears and a big, round nose clearly communicates "clown".

Create a:

man with short hair, closed eyes, small, straight nose, closed mouth, mustache, goatee

child with straight hair pulled back, bushy pigtails, almond-shaped eyes

man with round, fat face, curly hair, enormous eyes, small, pudgy nose, huge, open-mouthed smile

# The Total Look

This chapter provides you with the skills you need to add the finishing touches to any person in action that you wish to gesture. Observe the meaning of the facial expressions in the first two photographs below. You can combine these two facial expressions with the hand and finger configurations you use to represent people in action. You can combine the facial expressions in the second pair of photographs below with the hand and finger configurations you use to represent eye actions and reactions.

Use the facial expressions shown in the first four photographs on the opposite page to add meaning to the faces you create by gesturing their facial features. Copy and use each of the facial expressions below and on the following page.

**gracefully**

**awkwardly**

**peacefully**

**shocked**

Express the following:

dance gracefully
walk awkwardly
look peacefully
look shocked

The last two photographs below show facial expressions to add meaning to the clothes you gesture.

**beautiful**

**ugly**

**young**

**old**

Express these too:

young boy
old man
beautiful girl
ugly woman
sexy skirt
prim and proper blouse

**sexy**

prim and proper

# NOTES:

Chapter 8

# The More, the Merrier
Multiples of Objects and People

tacks, bunches, pairs, rows, groups and crowds; in other words, we often encounter more than one object or person at a time. You first practiced creating multiples in Chapter Two when you gestured two-dimensional dots, circles and squares. You can gesture multiples of objects using the same technique. Observe how to create two balls in a row.

You can also use the gesturing techniques you learned in Chapter Seven to create multiples of people. You used the index finger of one hand, for example, to represent one person from head to toe. Create the same gesture with both hands to create two people. Maintain the same hand shape on both hands, move your hands out to the sides and you create two more people—four in all. You can continue with this technique to create six people, then eight people, and so on.

If you are trying to visually communicate large groups of people, it is inefficient to begin with two people, add two, then two more, and so on. Instead, start with eight—the eight fingers of both hands. As you move your hands from the center outward you create eight more people, then eight more, and so on.

A common place to find long lines of people is at the entrance to some event. The special gesturing technique for this is to line your fingers up as if the people they represent were in line. Leave the first four people anchored at the beginning of the line as you move your other hand to show the length and direction of the rest of the line. Observe how the line of people stretches straight back and then turns to extend around the corner.

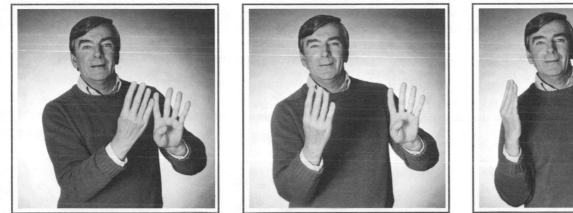

In Chapter Seven when you used hand shapes and finger configurations to represent people, you also enabled them to perform different kinds of action. You can show large groups of people performing the same action by using the eight fingers of both hands. Observe how to represent a row of fans sitting in the stands at a football game. By changing and repositioning your fingers, you can indicate how the fans rise and cheer for a touchdown. Adding the right facial expressions really makes the scene come alive.

Multiple ways of showing multiples prove the more, the merrier.

# The Shape of Things to Come

You gestured multiples of objects in Chapter Four when you put decorative balls on a Christmas tree and four wheels on a skateboard. When you placed the balls on the tree and the wheels on the skateboard you put them where they belonged, not stacked on top of each other. Observe in the photographs below how to gesture two cylinders. Notice how one cylinder is gestured to the left and one to the right to avoid stacking. Look at the first two photographs on the opposite page showing a horizontal cylinder. Where would you create the second cylinder to avoid stacking? Gesture multiples of the basic four shapes.

The remaining photographs opposite show a pyramid of milk bottles. Notice how the hand creating the first bottle remains in place as the other hand creates the second and third bottle in the first row.

Gesture:

icicles on the eaves of a roof
a stack of oranges
pillars of a colonial house
crates in a warehouse
bowling pins
books on a shelf
coins
jail bars
bull's horns
string of pearls
bunches of bananas
a checkerboard

After creating the fourth and fifth bottles, one hand stays on the second row while the other creates the top bottle.

Now gesture some items that contain more than one shape.

one triple-scoop ice cream cone

two cameras with zoom lenses

three birthday cakes with candles

10-, 20-, 30-, and 40 pound dumbbells

five TV sets with rabbit ears up

# Two by Two

Use the index fingers of both hands to create two people from head to toe instead of only one as in the first two photographs below. Show two fists to represent the heads and torsos of two people and the middle and index fingers of both hands to represent two people from the waist down as in the last two photographs below. You can show the two people you are representing in action by performing the action simultaneously on both hands. Move the index fingers of both hands outward and create four people from head to toe as in the first two photographs on the opposite page.

Observe in the other photographs on the opposite page how to create the heads and torsos of four people as well as their bodies from the waist down.

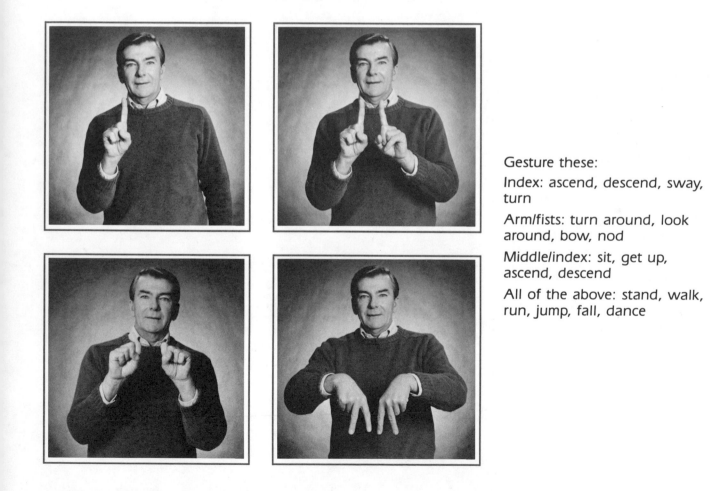

Gesture these:

Index: ascend, descend, sway, turn

Arm/fists: turn around, look around, bow, nod

Middle/index: sit, get up, ascend, descend

All of the above: stand, walk, run, jump, fall, dance

# More Power To You

Move the index fingers, fists, or middle and index fingers outward to create six, eight, and so on.

Gesture several people standing:

in a row

in a circle

in a semicircle

in each corner of the room

In several rows

behind each other on the stairs

# Plenty More Where That Came From

For larger numbers of people, don't waste time gesturing two by two. You can use the fingers of both hands to create eight or more people from head to toe or from waist to toe. You can show large numbers of people in action by performing the action simultaneously on both hands. The first two photographs below show how to represent eight or more people standing, then sitting. The second pair shows many people marching, perhaps in a parade. Notice how the proud facial expression reinforces the activity. Move the fingers of both hands outward and create eight more people from head to toe as in the first two photographs on the opposite page.

Observe in the remaining photographs on the opposite page how to create eight or more people from the waist down, standing and sitting.

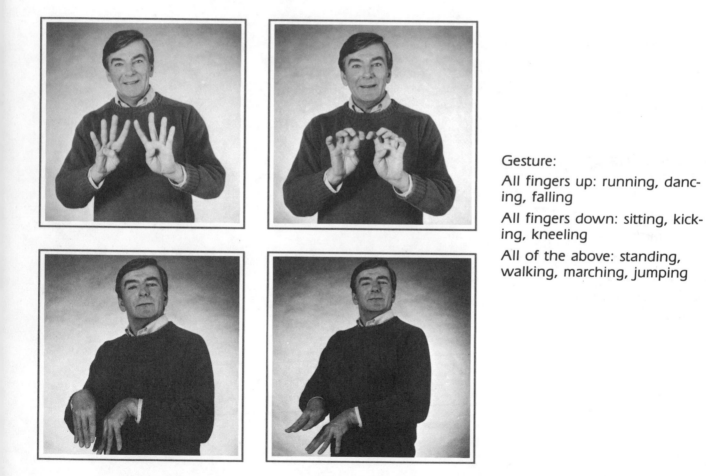

Gesture:

All fingers up: running, dancing, falling

All fingers down: sitting, kicking, kneeling

All of the above: standing, walking, marching, jumping

# Packing 'Em in Like Sardines

Continue to move your fingers outward and create twenty-four people, thirty-two people and so on.

Gesture many:

in a row

in a circle

in a semicircle

in several rows

behind each other on the stairs

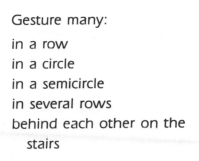

# Lined Up Around the Block

You can create any kind of line you want by using the gesturing technique for representing people in a line. Create the first people in line with one hand and the rest of the people with the other hand. Leave the first hand in place while stretching the second hand out to show the approximate length and shape of the line.

The photographs below show quite a long line that appears to make several sharp turns, perhaps around corners. The weary looking facial expression suggests that the people have been in this line for a long time and are tiring. Changing the facial expression to impatience, would add different meaning to the picture. Changing to anger would create an even different meaning. Think of other facial expressions that will change the gesture meaning.

Gesture people standing in a:

straight line

winding line

line weaving around the corner

line weaving over the landscape

# A Face in the Crowd

You can use the following facial expressions to add meaning to any of the multiple objects and people you gesture.

**patriotic**

**violent**

Express the following:

a patriotic stance
a violent runner
a festive dancer
a bored person in line
a plentiful amount of oranges
an unusual vase

**festive**

**bored**

**plentiful**

**unusual**

# NOTES:

# Chapter 9
# The Great Outdoors
## Nature and Its Inhabitants

n Chapter Nine you will create large panoramic scenes. You will also use techniques similar to those you learned in Chapter Seven to gesture the distinctive parts of animals and birds that inhabit natural scenes. Let's start with a familiar piece of nature: a valley. Can you picture it? View it as if the inclines from both sides of the valley come together right in front of you. First gesture the land from which the valley falls, then bring your hands down toward each other to create the depth of the valley. Let your hands meet to form the base of the valley.

In an outdoor scene, you can combine several aspects of nature. For example, imagine a scene in which the shining sun enables a flower to grow. You will want to create both the sun and the flower, as in the first photograph in the series below. After both the sun and the flower are in place, you can gesture the sun shining down on the flower. You might pick the flower and bring it up to your face to smell it, as in the final photograph below.

Later in this chapter you will practice creating natural scenes from the lava flow of an erupting volcano to the tranquil mystery of a desert oasis.

In Chapter Seven you learned to use hand shapes and finger configurations to represent parts of a person. There are accepted gestures for representing the distinctive parts of animals as well. Observe, for example, how to represent the paws of a lion using the fists of both hands. See how to gesture the lion's claws as it confronts a rival. After a successful defense of its territory, notice how to show off the lion's shaggy mane.

There are also accepted gestures for representing the parts of birds. Observe how to represent the clawed feet of an eagle, for example. You can gesture a bird's wingspan by creating the wings in front of your body and letting their distance from each other indicate the comparative size of the bird. Show its manner of flight by moving the arms appropriately.

Whether you're comfortable at camp or prefer the interior of a grand hotel, have fun with the following activities that take you into the great outdoors.

# Taking in the Scenery

You've learned to create objects, to create a scene, and to place objects within the scene. Now use all of these skills to create outdoor scenes. Begin by observing how to gesture calm and choppy water, contrasted in the two sets of photographs below. Notice how the movement of the hands and body communicates the difference between the two kinds of water conditions, although the hand shapes remain the same for both. Notice also how the facial expressions add meaning to the gestures and help to distinguish one concept from the other.

Now observe the contrasting photographs of smooth and rugged landscape in the first two photographs on the opposite page. Notice the meaning added by the facial expressions too. Incorporate also, the use of body position, some scenes can take place at an angle, to the side or in front of you.

Gesture this scenery:
a calm stream
river rapids
a calm lake
a waterfall
a calm ocean
a flood
a sand dune
a smooth hill
a rugged mountain
a smooth valley
a rugged canyon
an erupting volcano

The second pair of photographs contrasts a clear and dark sky, the final pair shows a dying, then a blazing, fire.

Gesture this scenery, too:
puffy clouds
haze
a thunderstorm
dense fog
a rainbow
the aurora borealis
a crackling fire
a cozy fire in a fireplace
a blazing forest fire
a bonfire
a lighted torch
a lighted candle

# A Bird in the Hand

Use the index and middle fingers and thumbs of both hands to represent the legs of a bird with clawed feet, standing, as in the first photograph below. Flattened hands represent the legs of a bird with webbed feet, standing or paddling as in the second and third photos. The fingers of both hands, palms out, represent a bird's wings.

As the first photograph on the opposite page shows, bent index fingers on both hands represent an animal standing on two legs. Next, the index and middle finger represent an animal standing on four longer legs. Third, bent index and middle fingers on both hands represent an animal with four short legs, standing. In the fourth photograph, fists facing down represent paws or hooves.

Represent birds in action:
a duck waddling
a flamingo standing
an owl catching a mouse
a goose flying
a hummingbird hovering
an ostrich running
an eagle gliding
a robin hopping

Claws about to attack and the extended index finger for
a tail are shown in the last two photos.

Gesture animals on the move:

an elephant swaying

a horse rearing up on hind
legs

a donkey kicking up its hind
legs

a cat attacking with its claws

a rabbit hopping

a deer prancing

a bear walking upright

a lion closing in on its prey

a dog sitting up on hind legs,
wagging its tail

a monkey swinging in a tree

# In Perfect Harmony

Create outdoor scenes using the natural scenery, animals and people you've practiced gesturing. Observe how to gesture the scene of a mountain under a dark, windy and rainy sky. Begin by gesturing the mountain. Notice how one hand remains in its original position at the base of the mountain as the other hand creates two mountain peaks.

Now create the weather conditions covering the mountain: overcast sky, wind and rain. On the opposite page, you first see the sky darkening. In the second photo, the storm approaches. In the third and fourth photos the open hands move from one side to another as the wind blows. Finally, the bent fingers of both hands move toward the ground showing the falling rain.

Gesture these outdoor scenes:
sunrise
shore, fog
hills, sunset, stars
meadow, pond, rainbow

Note how the facial expressions accompanying sky, wind and rain change and add to the communicated gestures.

Now gesture these:
mountain, snow, wind
volcano eruption, lava flow
river, ripples, rapids, waterfall
desert, palm trees, spring,
man drinking water

# In Perfect Harmony (continued)

Now the weather is about to make a change for the better. Watch as the sky clears and a rainbow stretches across the sky. A bird appears and perches on the tree. Notice how the sky is gestured before the rainbow since the rainbow appears in the sky. The tree is gestured before the bird because the bird must perch on one of the branches, and to do so, the tree must already be there. Observe how the face brightens with the improved weather adding to the clarity of the communication.

Can you think of any scenery to add to this scene—any other pleasant conditions or animals or birds? Perhaps a butterfly floats over the tree or a squirrel climbs up it. Include the skills of directionality and perspective from previous chapters and add those techniques to the scene.

Gesture these scenes:

a corn field, river, rain, lightning, and a tornado

a cliff, an ocean with waves, puffy clouds, a midday sun and a seagull

a woman walking over rocky ground, a geyser spraying water and a moose standing nearby

night, a full moon, woods, a campfire and children sitting

# Looking Natural

Notice the meaning each of the following facial expressions communicates. Then copy them yourself.

**bright**

**dark**

**timid**

**proud**

Express the following:
"bright" day
"dark" day
"tame" horse
"wild" lion
"timid" rabbit
"proud" eagle

**tame**

**wild**

# NOTES:

Chapter 10

# The Best Story I've Ever Seen

Storytelling

**B**y combining gesture, mime and facial expression—the fundamentals of American Sign Language—you will be able to tell a story from beginning to end. Whether your story is once upon a time or some future time the additional techniques presented will make your storytelling effective as well as entertaining.

Storytelling begins by distinguishing between past, present and future actions. Indicate past action by moving your hand backwards, as in the first photograph below; present, by pulling your hands down in front of your body; and future, by moving your hand forward, as in the third photograph.

Before you relate a story, visualize it and plan its presentation. Begin by setting the stage. Where is the action happening? Do any important props need to be gestured such as the beans and the axe in the story of "Jack and the Beanstalk?"

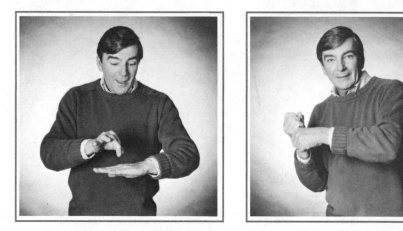

Be prepared to gesture any additional props that you need to clearly tell your story when they first become important to the story line.

Create the cast of characters as they are introduced into the story. Gesture each character's prominent physical attributes and clothes. Select one of these attributes to tell your audience which character is doing the action. For example, you might indicate Jack by standing bravely. You could clench your fists in anger and put an evil look on your face to indicate the Giant. Help the viewer understand which character is doing the action by shifting your body position so that each character faces a different direction.

Your facial expressions will provide important information in the story. The first photograph below indicates that our hero, Jack, is in some kind of trouble. But Jack's expression in the second photograph shows that he doesn't like to be pushed around. After Jack chops down the beanstalk with his axe, the Giant plummets to the ground and we can see that Jack is aghast at the sight. Be creative and add to the story.

Combine these storytelling techniques with everything else you have learned and practiced to show us the best story we've ever seen.

# The Man of a Thousand Faces

That's what they called silent film star Lon Chaney, the son of deaf parents. He could communicate a great deal without words, using facial expressions and natural gestures, and you can too. Observe how to act out the classic melodrama, "I Can't Pay the Rent" using facial expressions and gestures to play the heroine, the villain and the hero.

Notice how the storyteller is able to communicate exactly which character he is portraying. He looks helpless and distressed as he plays the heroine; mean and unrelenting as he plays the villain; and courageous and forthright as he plays the hero. As you perform this short melodrama yourself, playing each part, let your face and gestures help to communicate which character you are portraying.

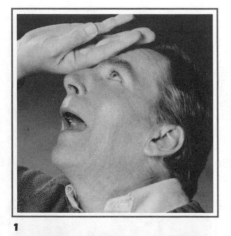

1

2

3

4

1. **Heroine:** "I can't pay the rent."
2. **Villain:** "You must pay the rent."
3. **Hero:** "I'll pay the rent."
4. **Heroine:** "My hero!"

# Striving to Build Your Character

Observe how to show the eyes, teeth, ears and snout of the big bad wolf from the story, "Little Red Riding Hood".

Gesture the following characters:

Dumbo

Humpty Dumpty

Snow White

Bugs Bunny

Superman

Frankenstein

Roadrunner

Popeye

Mickey Mouse

# That's Entertainment

Begin your storytelling practice with a familiar story such as the tale of Dr. Jekyll and Mr. Hyde in which the good Dr. Jekyll is tranformed into the hideous Mr. Hyde by drinking an evil potion. Pay close attention to facial expressions and the important meaning they communicate. Notice in the first two photographs below how calm and composed the gentle Dr. Jekyll is at first as he checks his formula and takes the beakers into his hands. Then, his excitement builds as he prepares to drink the potion.

The photographs on the opposite page show how excitement changes to terror as the formula begins to take effect. Finally the gruesome Mr. Hyde emerges. As you present this tale add some terrifying details. Perhaps you will prey upon an unsuspecting victim.

Gesture the following stories:

Snow White and the Seven Dwarfs

Cinderella

Jack and the Beanstalk

The Three Little Pigs

As you let Mr. Hyde gain full control, include the hate and rage on his face as in the last photos below.

Try these stories too:
Hansel and Gretel
Pinocchio
Alice in Wonderland
Rapunzel

# Double Feature

In our second storytelling feature observe how to gesture the humorous sequence of events of a man who slips on a banana peel that someone else throws down. The story begins as one of our characters peels, eats and carelessly tosses the remains of his midday snack. The action of the story alternates between its two characters: the person who tosses the banana peel and the person who slips on it. Since "slipping on the peel" is difficult and certainly dangerous to act out, the index and middle fingers are used to represent the person doing that action.

The last two photographs on the opposite page show how the man who slipped also hurt his head. The first fellow appears to be enjoying the other man's misfortune, perhaps unaware that he is the cause.

Gesture these stories:

Goldilocks and the Three Bears

Little Red Riding Hood

Peter Pan

Rip Van Winkle

The position of the body and the logic of the story make it clear which man hurt his head and which is laughing.

Try these modern tales:
Raiders of the Lost Ark
Rocky
Romancing the Stone
Superman

# The Best Story I've Ever Seen

Ladies and gentlemen! For our final gestured story, we invite you to witness the courage and daring of the man with nerves of steel. Can he do it? Can you? Watch him as he dives into a pool of water from a death-defying height. Notice from the look on his face that he has some concerns about what he is about to do.

Since the flow of this story is unfamiliar to most people, the storyteller must take special care to provide the viewer with all the information needed to understand the story. Therefore, notice how he even gestures his own ladder before beginning his climb. Watch as he stands on the platform, with the index and middle fingers representing this action, as he overcomes his trepidation and starts his dive. Notice not only the facial expression, but also the change in direction of the head.

Watch as he plummets, head first, past the rungs of the ladder into the water—causing water to spray up.

Use your storytelling skills on these:

a personal story

an unusual event

a children's story

a movie

a TV program

a news report

a weather report

a gossip story

an unbelievable tabloid story

# NOTES:

# The Design of a Sign

## Creating Signs from Gestures, Mime and Facial Expressions

f you have successfully learned the skills leading to this chapter, you have also learned the fundamentals of American Sign Language. In the process of learning these skills, you have also acquired a sizable sign language vocabulary... one that was derived from your gesturing vocabulary. The signs for some nouns are derived from one or more of their physical characteristics or how they are handled or used. If you gesture the roof and two sides of a house, you've produced the sign for "house." The sign for "baby" is conveyed by gesturing a baby being held, instead of its physical characteristics.

The signs for some verbs are derived from their mimed action or by hand representation of their action. When you bring your hand up to your mouth to gesture eat, you are producing the sign for "eat." Using the middle and index fingers to gesture "stand" is the sign for "stand" as well.

The signs for some verbs include some gestured objects. Combining the object, wall, with the action of painting, is the sign for "paint," as in the last photograph above. Notice also, in the sign for "stand", the gestured flat hand is the object or floor.

Some signs represent abstract concepts. You can represent "morning" as a gesturing sequence of the sun coming up over the horizon, the sign for "morning" is shown in the first two photographs below.

Signs can also represent other abstract concepts of size, quality, condition and age. In the last photograph above, the concrete representation of the concept, such as shivering, is paired with an appropriate facial expression to convey the complete meaning of the sign: "cold".

Not all actions are visible. However, visible actions are used to represent the signs for process verbs. You can't watch someone "think," but you can represent it by pointing to the mind working. Combine "think" with the sign for "same" and the result is the sign for "agree," as in the complete series below.

Add all of your skills using gesture, mime and facial expression to your skills in sign and you will have all the communication tools "from mime to sign". With these skills you will clearly be able to understand the design of a sign.

# Gesture-Sign Connection #1

## The signs for some nouns are derived from their physical characteristics.

### Ball

Gesture the ball shape.

### Balloon

Show it getting bigger as you blow it up.

### Box

Gesture the box shape.

### House

Show the roof and two side walls.

### Floor
Show its area by extending one hand forward.

### Wall
Show its length by extending both hands sideways.

### Door
Show it closed, then open it.

### Window
Show it rising off its sill.

### Tree

Show it standing on the ground, using your arm and fingers to represent the trunk and branches.

### Mountain

Show its base, then its peak.

### Valley

Show its height, then its depth.

### Fire

Show the flames leaping and flickering upward.

### Cloud

Form its puffy shape.

### Ocean

Show the size and movement of its waves.

### River

Show a narrower flow of water.

### Sky

Show its location by extending both hands upward and outward.

**Rain**

Show the drops pelt the ground.

**Snow**

Show the flakes drift toward the ground.

**Wind**

Show it blowing back and forth.

**Rainbow**

Show it arch across the sky.

### Child
Show an appropriate height.

### Girl
Show the ribbon of her bonnet + her height.

### Boy
Show the brim of his cap + his height.

### Woman
Show the ribbon of her bonnet + her height.

**Man**

Show the brim of his hat + his height.

**Elephant**

Show its long trunk.

**Cat**

Show its whiskers.

**Lion**

Show its shaggy mane.

### Turtle

Show its head sticking out from under its shell.

### Bird

Show its straight beak opening and closing.

### Butterfly

Show its wings fluttering in flight.

### Fish

Show it swimming as its tail propels it through the water.

# Gesture-Sign Connection #2

**The signs for some nouns are derived from how they are handled or used.**

**Bread**

Show a loaf and slice it.

**Sandwich**

Show the outside slices of bread and eat it.

**Soup**

Eat the soup from the bowl with a spoon.

**Egg**

Crack the shell open.

### Ice Cream
Lick the scoop on the cone.

### Banana
Peel it.

### Corn
Eat the kernels off the ear.

### Onion
Rub away the tears it causes.

**Baby**

Rock the baby back and forth in your arms.

**Dog**

Call it by tapping your leg and snapping your fingers.

**Car**

Rotate the steering wheel back and forth.

**Flower**

Bring it to your nose and smell it.

# Gesture-Sign Connection #3

**The signs for some verbs are derived from their mimed action.**

**Hear**

Point to your ear.

**Taste**

Bring one finger sampling food to your mouth.

**Smell**

Direct the fragrance toward your nose.

**Touch**

Bring one finger to a solid surface.

## Move

Position your hands as if placing a rug in a new location.

## Carry

Position your hands as if loaded down with a watermelon.

## Drop

Do this activity as if something slipped out of your hands.

## Pick Up

Reach down and lift it up as if finding a ten dollar bill.

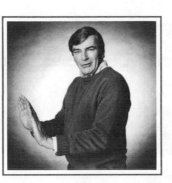

**Push**

Show the exertion against a flat surface.

**Pull**

Show the action of tug of war.

**Give**

Gesture this activity as if delivering a letter.

**Receive**

Extend your hands as if grasping an award.

**Throw**

Move one hand forward as if tossing a set of keys.

**Swim**

Move your hands as if pulling yourself through the water.

**Fish**

Move both hands forward as if casting a line.

**Climb**

Do this action as if ascending a ladder.

## Wash

Act as if laundering a pair of socks.

## Dig

Move down and back as if shoveling dirt.

## Sew

Move one hand up and down as if pulling a needle and thread through fabric.

## Eat

Bring one hand carrying food to the mouth.

# Gesture-Sign Connection #4

## The signs for some verbs include mimed action and gestured objects.

### Show

Form a display and show it while moving it forward.

### Compare

Display two similar objects move and compare them.

### Build

Place one brick upon another.

### Connect

Form two links of a chain and connect them.

### Draw
Form a canvas and draw on it.

### Write
Form a pad and write on it.

### Paint
Form a wall and paint on it.

### Drink
Form a cup and drink from it.

### Bake

Form a pan and slide it into the oven.

### Cook

Form food and cook it on both sides.

### Marry

Join two hands together.

### Cry

Form tears coming down your cheeks.

### Open

Form two closed doors and open them.

### Close

Form two open doors and close them.

### Increase

Form a spoon and increase the quantity by one spoonful.

### Decrease

Form a spoon and decrease the quantity by one spoonful.

# Gesture-Sign Connection #5

**The signs for some verbs are derived from hand representations for actions.**

### Stand

Use the index and middle fingers to represent a person from waist to toe "standing."

### Get Up

Use the index and middle fingers to represent a person from waist to toe "getting up."

### Lie Down

Use the index and middle fingers to represent a person from waist to toe "lying down."

### Jump

Use the index and midddle fingers to represent a person from waist to toe "jumping."

### Sit

Use the index and middle fingers to represent a person from waist to toe "sitting."

### Dance

Use the index and middle fingers to represent a person from waist to toe "dancing."

### Slide

Use the index and middle fingers to represent a person from waist to toe "sliding."

### Fall

Use the index and middle fingers to represent a person from waist to toe "falling."

### Nod

Use the arm and fist to represent the head and torso of a person "nodding."

### Walk

Use the palms of both hands to represent the feet of a person "walking."

### Appear

Use the index finger to represent a person from head to toe "appearing."

### Disappear

Use the index finger to represent a person from head to toe "disappearing."

### Escape

Use the index finger to represent a person from head to toe "escaping."

### Meet

Use the index fingers of both hands to represent people from head to toe "meeting."

### Line Up

Use all eight fingers of both hands to represent eight or more people from head to toe "lined up."

### March

Use all eight fingers of both hands to represent eight or more people from head to toe "marching."

# Gesture-Sign Connection #6

**The signs for some verbs are derived from hand representations for eye actions.**

### Squint

Compress the thumbs and index fingers of both hands to represent the eyes "squinting."

### See

With palm in, extend the index and middle fingers of one hand to represent the eyes "seeing."

### Look

Point the index and middle fingers of one hand out to represent the eyes "looking."

### Wake up

Expand the thumbs and index fingers of both hands moderately to represent the eyes "waking up."

## Surprise

Expand the thumbs and index fingers of both hands broadly to represent the eyes showing "surprise."

## Shock

Expand two clenched fists into semicircles to represent the eyes showing "shock."

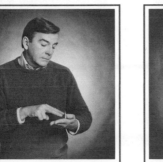 

## Read

Point the index and middle finger of one hand and move it along your palm to represent eyes "reading."

## Peek

Point the index and middle finger of one hand and move it from behind your other hand to represent eyes "peeking."

# Gesture-Sign Connection #7

**The signs for some abstract nouns are represented by visible objects or actions.**

### Time

Point to the wrist where your watch would be.

### Past

Indicate the time that is already behind you.

### Present

Indicate the time that is right in front of you.

### Future

Indicate the time that is still ahead of you.

### Minute

Show the movement of one minute on the face of a clock by letting the minute hand tick once.

### Morning

Show the sun coming up over the horizon.

### Noon

Show the sun straight up in the sky.

### Night

Show the sun going down over the horizon.

### Afternoon

Show the sun past noon.

**Day**

Show the sun moving through the sky from sunrise to sunset.

**Week**

Indicate one line of one month on a calendar.

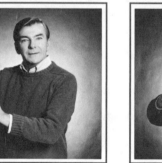 

**Month**

Indicate the row of weeks of one month on a calendar.

**Year**

Show the movement of the earth revolving around the sun.

### Spring

Show seasonal rebirth through a plant growing.

### Summer

Show the seasonal heat by wiping the sweat off your brow.

### Fall

Show the end of the growing season by harvesting crops as you chop them away.

### Winter

Show the seasonal cold by shivering.

# Gesture-Sign Connection #8

## The signs for some modifiers are represented by visible objects or actions.

### Small

Show the relative size of a small object.

### Big

Show the relative size of a big object.

### Light

Show the ease of carrying a light load.

### Heavy

Show the strain of carrying a heavy load.

### Soft

Show the flexibility of soft material.

### Hard

Show the inflexibility of a hard material.

### Light

Show the brightness of a cheerful, light day opening above you.

### Dark

Show the gloominess of a dark day coming down on you.

**Cold**

Show the natural reaction to weather that is too cold.

**Hot**

Show the natural reaction to eating food that is too hot by removing it from your mouth.

**Young**

Show the energy of youth as your exuberance moves up your torso.

**Old**

Show the fatigue and beard of an old man.

### Thin

Show the drawn, sunken look of extreme thinness.

### Fat

Show the full, puffy look of obesity.

### Happy

Show the natural reaction to happiness by bringing your positive feelings up and to the surface.

### Sad

Show the natural "long-faced" reaction to sadness.

### Brave

Show the strength and determination of braveness that you grasp from within.

### Frightened

Show the weakness and trembling of fright.

### Same

Use your index fingers to show the similarity of two objects.

### Different

Separate your index fingers to show the difference between two objects.

# Gesture-Sign Connection #9

**The signs for some verbs indicating mental activity are represented by visible objects or actions.**

### Think

Show the mind working.

### Remember

Show a thought being retrieved and staying with you.

### Forget

Show the mind being wiped clean.

### Dream

Show a thought floating into the air.

**Know**

Show information within the head.

**Understand**

Show a lightbulb going on.

**Misunderstand**

Show a thought being turned around within the head.

**Invent**

Show thoughts coming from within the mind.

### Learn

Show knowledge that is taken from a book and put into the mind.

### Teach

Show knowledge being taken from the mind and put into another person.

### Inform

Show information being given to others.

### Judge

Show evidence being weighed on the scales of justice.

 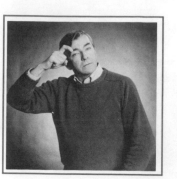

### Wise

Show a deep amount of knowledge.

### Puzzled

Show a question with a gestured question mark coming from the mind.

### Smart

Show bountiful intelligence rising from the mind.

### Stupid

Show a thick skull.

# Gesture-Sign Connection #10

**The signs for some nouns and verbs combine two independent signs.**

**Wife**

Woman + Marry

**Husband**

Man + Marry

**Mother**

Woman + (showing) Baby

**Father**

Man + (showing) Baby

## Grandmother

Mother + (showing) Baby

### Daughter

Girl + (holding) Baby

## Son

Boy + (holding) Baby

**Sister**

Girl + Same

**Brother**

Boy + Same

**Agree**

Think + Same

**Believe**

Think + Marry

**Decide**

Think + Judge

**Breakfast**

Eat + Morning

**Lunch**

Eat + Noon

**Dinner**

Eat + Night

# Big Picture

Apply all of your signing and gesturing skills by translating the following sentences and stories into signs and gestures.

A boy is sitting under a tree.

A boy is sitting on a hard box.

A dog is sleeping under a tree.

A man and a woman are walking up a mountain

Mother received a bouquet of flowers from the little girl.

At noon, many clouds are in the sky.

A frightened monkey is climbing a tree.

A beautiful girl is walking along the ocean.

A baby is crying all day.

A fish is swimming down a river.

A girl finds a flower that is laying on top of the snow.

A big ball is on a hard box. A little girl sees the ball. The girl kicks the ball off the box. The girl jumps over the box. The girl falls, gets up, and cries. The girl walks to a tree and sits under the tree. Mother is inside the house and sees the girl crying. Mother walks outside to the girl. Mother gives the girl a balloon on a string. The girl becomes happy.

A brave boy walks up to the door of a big, old house. The boy pushes the door open. The boy walks inside and looks around. An ugly old man suddenly appears from behind the door. The boy is frightened and runs out the door away from the house.

A boy writes on the wall inside a house. The boy is happy. Mother walks in and sees the boy writing on the wall. Mother is shocked. The boy is surprised. Mother and the boy wash the wall.

An old woman sees a small cat in the snow. The cat is very cold. The old woman is sad. The woman carries the cat to her house. The woman places the cat in a box on the floor. The cat sleeps in the box on the floor. The woman watches the cat. The woman is very happy.

# NOTES:

# Index

Signs, vocabulary (cont'd)

| | | | | |
|---|---|---|---|---|
| corn | 143 | learn | 171 | |
| cry | 152 | light (bright) | 165 | |
| dance | 155 | light (weight) | 164 | |
| dark | 165 | line up | 157 | |
| daughter | 174 | lion | 140 | |
| day | 162 | look | 158 | |
| decide | 176 | lunch | 176 | |
| decrease | 153 | man | 140 | |
| different | 168 | march | 157 | |
| dig | 149 | marry | 152 | |
| dinner | 176 | meet | 157 | |
| disappear | 156 | minute | 161 | |
| dog | 144 | misunderstand | 170 | |
| door | 135 | month | 162 | |
| draw | 151 | morning | 161 | |
| dream | 169 | mother | 173 | |
| drink | 151 | mountain | 136 | |
| drop | 146 | move | 146 | |
| eat | 149 | night | 161 | |
| egg | 142 | nod | 156 | |
| elephant | 140 | noon | 161 | |
| escape | 157 | ocean | 137 | |
| fall (noun) | 163 | old | 166 | |
| fall (verb) | 155 | onion | 143 | |
| fat | 167 | open | 153 | |
| father | 173 | paint | 151 | |
| fire | 136 | past | 160 | |
| fish (noun) | 141 | peek | 159 | |
| fish (verb) | 148 | pick up | 146 | |
| floor | 135 | present (now) | 160 | |
| flower | 144 | pull | 147 | |
| forget | 169 | push | 147 | |
| frightened | 168 | puzzled | 172 | |
| future | 160 | rain | 138 | |
| get up | 154 | rainbow | 138 | |
| girl | 139 | read | 159 | |
| give | 147 | receive | 147 | |
| grandmother | 174 | remember | 169 | |
| happy | 167 | river | 137 | |
| hard | 165 | sad | 167 | |
| hear | 145 | same | 168 | |
| heavy | 164 | sandwich | 142 | |
| hot | 166 | see | 158 | |
| house | 134 | sew | 149 | |
| husband | 173 | shock | 159 | |
| ice cream | 143 | show | 150 | |
| increase | 153 | sister | 175 | |
| inform | 171 | sit | 155 | |
| invent | 170 | sky | 137 | |
| judge | 171 | slide | 155 | |
| jump | 154 | small | 164 | |
| know | 170 | smart | 172 | |
| lay down | 154 | smell | 145 | |
| | | snow | 138 | |

# A NOTE ABOUT THE VIDEOTAPES

A set of three corresponding videotapes is available for this book. The tapes provide an additional opportunity to enhance your progress and understanding. They are designed to reinforce concepts and skills you develop in the book.

For those who are interested in seeking feedback about their performance of the activities or for those who would like to see what the content of this book looks like in motion, you may want to obtain the videotapes. For best results in using the videos, it is recommended that the videos be viewed while referring to the book. This is necessary because the book provides the specific instruction you will need.

The videotapes are available as a set of three tapes or can be purchased individually.

| | |
|---|---|
| Videotape Part I Chapters 1-5 (45 min.) | **$89.95** |
| Videotape Part II Chapters 6-9 (50 min.) | **$89.95** |
| Videotape Part III Chapters 10-11 (45 min.) | **$89.95** |
| Special Price for set | **$229.95** |

You may notice some variations when comparing the tapes to the book. This is a result of transferring mediums. Still, the basic progression of skills and Gil Eastman's natural approach are presented in a way which we hope gets you feeling even more confident and comfortable with your visual-gestural communication.

For more information about the videotapes or to order, contact:

T.J. Publishers, Inc.
817 Silver Spring Avenue
Suite 206
Silver Spring, MD 20910
(301) 585-4440 CUSTOMER SERVICE
800-999-1168 (V/TDD) ORDERS ONLY!
301-585-5930 FAX ORDERS